John F. alexander

YOUR MONEY OR YOUR LIFE

YOUR MONEY
OR YOUR LIFE

A New Look at Jesus'
View of Wealth and Power

John F. Alexander

1817

Harper & Row, Publishers, San Francisco

Cambridge, Hagerstown, New York, Philadelphia, Washington
London, Mexico City, São Paulo, Singapore, Sydney

Portions of this work have appeared in somewhat different form in *The Other Side*, a monthly magazine for Christians concerned about justice and discipleship, 300 W. Apsley Street, Philadelphia, PA 19144. Material adapted by permission.

YOUR MONEY OR YOUR LIFE. © 1986 by John Alexander. All rights reserved. Printed in the United States of America. No part of this book may be used or reproduced in any manner whatsoever without written permission except in the case of brief quotations embodied in critical articles and reviews. For information address Harper & Row, Publishers, Inc., 10 East 53rd Street, New York, N.Y. 10022. Published simultaneously in Canada by Fitzhenry & Whiteside Limited, Toronto.

FIRST EDITION

Library of Congress Cataloging-in-Publication Data
Alexander, John F.
    Your money or your life.

    1. Jesus Christ—Teachings. 2. Wealth—Biblical
teaching. 3. Power (Christian theology)—Biblical
teaching. 4. Christian life—1960–   . I. Title.
BS2417.W4A44   1986   248.4   86-45010
ISBN 0-06-060151-5

86 87 88 89 90 RRD 10 9 8 7 6 5 4 3 2 1

To my father, Fred Alexander.

His sermons on discipleship (Luke 14:25–33), preached when I was a kid, are the basis of this book. He is an unusual fundamentalist; for he believes that inerrancy extends to the teachings of Jesus.

Contents

Acknowledgments

I would like to thank Raficq Abdullah for the encouragement he gave me to write this book, even though he knew he would disagree with much of what I wrote. And I would like to thank Marianne for being my friend and the friend of my family while I was writing.

I would like to thank Louis Turner and Jean Carr for allowing my family and me to live in their home in London while I wrote part of this book, even though they think that most of what I wrote is positively bizarre.

I would like to thank Joe Comanda, whose critique of the first few chapters has had a lasting effect on my style.

I would like to thank Joe Peterson and the folks at Shiloh for the cabin they provided for us to live in while I wrote another part of this book. I would also like to thank Joe for reinforcing my beliefs at a time when they seemed crazy even to me and for his expressing those beliefs in trenchant ways—many of which found their way into this book.

I would like to thank Gretchen Williver who typed the entire manuscript for no pay at a time when we had never even met.

I would like to thank my wife for tolerating me while I went through the agonies of writing this book; she practiced being a suffering servant when I was merely writing about it. More important, I would like to thank her for being my intellectual partner: what is printed here are her ideas nearly as much as mine.

I would especially like to thank *The Other Side* magazine for giving me a year's sabbatical with pay while I wrote this book.

1. INSANITY AND REPENTANCE

1. I Don't Understand

To tell you the truth, I don't understand. We live in a world of wonder, but we have made it a sickening mess.

Forty thousand children will die today because they are poor,[1] and nuclear war could annihilate us all at any moment. This week the papers are full of pictures of people in Beirut who have been burned by phosphorous bombs. People are being tortured right now in Korea, the Soviet Union, El Salvador, South Africa, Uganda, and three dozen other countries. And . . . .

We have made hell while the stars shine beautifully.

But that's not what I don't understand. What I don't understand is that we more or less accept it.

Perhaps I would understand accepting it if we were enjoying ourselves, but we aren't. Half the people I know are going through messy divorces, and half are killing themselves with cigarettes. Surrounded by flowers and human beings and cathedrals, we watch TV (which bores us) and joke about the rat race. Meanwhile, we take valium (it is hard to sleep in hell) and try not to notice the pain.

The world's attention was held by the mass suicide Jim Jones led in Guyana, but we scarcely notice the mass death of poor kids or our own unsatisfactory lives.

Meanwhile we get up in the morning, drink our coffee, go to work, come home, eat dinner, put the kids to bed, watch TV, lock up, and go to bed. Maybe after dinner we send a check to save the children; maybe over the weekend we go to church or even to a demonstration. But we do not let the horrors of the world disturb our routine. We do not even find time to meditate or to feel how those kids are dying.

In other words, we carry on with business as usual, "selling ice boxes on the burning deck. . . . While the roads are deep with the corpses of every sane and beautiful thing."[2]

You'd think we'd do something. I would understand pouring blood at the Pentagon. I would understand quitting one's job and joining a convent to devote one's life to prayer. I would understand trying to get the president of the United States committed to an insane asylum. I would certainly understand retiring to the woods. I would even understand throwing bombs (though I wouldn't accept it).

But I do not understand carrying on—selling ice boxes on the burning deck. You'd think people would find some way to say no to hell, some way to say yes to life. But we don't even seem to notice.

It does not have to be this way. We *can* choose otherwise. And we sometimes do. We can choose truth and beauty and people.

Remember the sunset? Remember the hard work that finally yielded some insight? Remember the child's smile? Remember God? We can still remember, just barely.

So why do we make such bad choices? I don't understand.

I especially don't understand Christians. Not that we're worse than anyone else, but Christianity promises so much and we deliver so little.

I used to say that Christians spend half their time explaining why Jesus couldn't possibly have meant what he clearly said, but I'm afraid I was mistaken. We Christians don't have to explain away what Jesus said; we simply don't notice it in the first place.

Jesus talked about loving God with your whole being (which is beyond imagining) and loving your neighbor as yourself. He talked about taking up your cross, about giving your cloak as well as your coat, about going a second mile, and about loaning to those who ask. He told us to exchange all for a pearl of great price and leave concern for our food and clothing to God. But we just carry on.

In *The Warden* by Anthony Trollope, a clergyman gives up a handsome living because he believes the income was intended for the poor. His clergyman son-in-law asks him how he'll survive, and he responds, "God, that feeds the young ravens, will take care of me also." "Pish," responds his son-in-law.[3]

William Neil gives a response that is more sophisticated, but it comes to the same thing: "We can see . . . that Jesus does not mean his hearers to take him literally." For if a man gave his cloak as well as his coat, that "would of course leave the man naked except for his loincloth!" And going a second mile is "obviously the last thing a conscript would dream of doing." As for loaning to all comers, "To obey this literally would encourage spongers, and reward the shiftless and thriftless at the expense of those working for a living. Jesus is obviously not commending indiscriminate charity, which is demoralizing."[4]

Well . . .

Perhaps Jesus didn't mean his teachings literally, but he surely meant us to have a passionate faith, a burning concern for people, and a flagrant disregard for our own rights and possessions. And while you can hardly expect that much from organized religion, you'd think individual Christians would show more regard for their roots. You'd think we'd interrupt our schedules long enough to say no to a world where torture is routine, no to a world where starving is routine. You'd think Christians would weep—or something. But in fact we aren't easy to distinguish from our secular neighbors.

Which is what I don't understand. Christian faith is lovely, awful, enormous, all-encompassing, demanding, wonderful, terrible, threatening, exciting. It rolls on and on without end. It has the hugeness and power of a blizzard. Yet somehow we manage to turn it into ice cubes to store in the freezer for later use.

Let's be honest. How many of us love God with our whole being? Aren't we too busy earning a living or keeping house? And how often do we turn the other cheek—literally *or* metaphorically? Or care about the world in any proportion to its suffering? We have settled for maybe 30 percent of Christianity, and some of that we've got out of focus. We've settled for a few scraps.

But we could have so much more.

It's not that I can't understand people saying "Pish" to Jesus. I understand that perfectly. After all, Jesus hinders our pursuit of our self-interest. What I don't understand is *Christians* saying "Pish" to Jesus. I don't understand Christians carrying on with business as usual—selling ice boxes as if the deck weren't burning, as if they weren't Christian.

Perhaps I am being too harsh, but I wish such people would admit that they simply have no intention of following Jesus. I could understand that. But I suppose people don't work that way. We prefer to kid ourselves, to pretend we're Christian— while carrying on our dispassionate routine, and clinging to our rights and possessions.

It's not that I expect Christians to live up to Jesus' way. We can't begin to do that—at least I can't. But we can try. We can begin the journey. What baffles me is people who reject the route and call themselves Christian.

Sometimes I think such people are being hypocritical or even cynical. Maybe calling themselves Christian helps their business or something—which may be true for some television evangelists or politicians. But most people who call themselves Christian seem quite sincere. They just haven't noticed the contradiction between their lives and their confession.

Which is what I don't understand.

I suspect that the hell we have made is connected with the failure of Christians to remember what they're about. The phosphorous bombs being dropped are related to people rejecting the very idea of turning the other cheek. Unsatisfactory lives and starving kids are related to our refusal to detach ourselves from our possessions.

Christians are not completely unconcerned about the horrors in the world, of course. Many are very active and have done a great deal of good. Think, for example, of the hospitals, orphanages, development agencies, and lobbying efforts led by Christians. But even the response of these Christians is often less rooted in the way of Christ than in a pragmatic "Pish."

Thus Christians fighting hunger usually see it as a technological problem requiring more money, more research, and more education for the poor. Some *do* see it as a matter of political and economic justice, but very few see it as a moral and spiritual problem connected to a deeper human hunger rooted in us all. Without noticing that they are doing it, well-meaning Christians replace repentance and contemplation with fund raising and irrigation.

And those of us working for peace are not necessarily concerned about whether we are at peace with our opponents, our fellow workers, or ourselves. We do not understand that peace comes from within. And more serious yet, some Christians (probably a majority) think that the way to peace is through a balance of power. It does not occur to them to ask if a balance of power is the way of the cross.

In short, Christians operate mostly in the pragmatic realm of money and power. If we want to lead a full life, we expect to spend a lot of money. If we want to reform the world, we try to do it by using money and power. It does not occur to us that the realm of darkness could better be resisted by the weapons of another realm—by servanthood, weakness, prayer, and truth. For we fight not against flesh and blood.

But we modern people are not resisting darkness or fighting evil; we are working for progress, and we will do so comfortably, negotiating from strength. The suffering servant is a religious oddity, from another realm. So we reject that realm, thereby choosing shallowness and perpetuating hollowness.

But for people concerned for the world or themselves, for people who sense the inadequacy of our pragmatic efforts at improvement, wisdom from another realm deserves to be explored—at least by Christians. Encouraging that exploration is what this book is about.

2. Insanity

During the Vietnam war, a group of protesters were arrested in Chicago. I think they had poured blood on draft records. At the trial, they entered a plea of insanity. They argued that legally a person is insane who can't tell right from wrong while committing a crime. And when they poured the blood they had no idea they were doing anything wrong. In fact, they thought it was the people dropping napalm on children who were doing wrong. So apparently, the defendants argued, they couldn't tell right from wrong; apparently they were insane. To them it seemed clear that people like Richard Nixon and Lyndon Johnson were war criminals, while draft resisters and war protesters were only doing their civic duty.

For many years that insanity plea was a parable for my life, and in some ways it still is. I hesitate to use it publicly for fear it will sound like radical chic, but I do not know how else to express the enormity of the chasm between reality and our perception of it. And indeed I often genuinely feel that somebody is insane: either me or the broadcaster who reads out the day's horrors so equably.

I mean, suppose a passenger ship was on fire and was about to capsize; suppose that if the fire didn't get the passengers, the water would. And suppose one man, a passenger, wasn't scrambling to put on a life preserver and neither was he helping other passengers. He was selling ice boxes on the burning deck. What would you think? Wouldn't you think he had lost touch with reality? Wouldn't you think he was crazy?

Well, people are being tortured, kids are starving, the bomb could be dropped any time, and we maintain our routine as if nothing were happening. I find that peculiar. We're out of touch with vast chunks of reality.

In fact, we're crazy.

Ah, but you may say I've overstated my case. Doomsayers like me are always announcing disasters that never strike. We shouldn't cry wolf so often. The end of the world never comes; the ship never sinks.

But disaster *has* struck. People are being tortured and killed. If that doesn't seem like the end of the world to us, it is only because it is not happening to us—we are not being tortured, and our kids are not among the forty thousand.

Let me ask you something. Had doom struck when Hitler was killing the Jews? If you think it had, do you realize that Hitler's gas chambers and crematoria couldn't handle forty thousand a day? It took him years to kill six million Jews; poverty kills that many kids every five months or so.[1] With Jews we call it the holocaust. With kids we don't even bother to name it. We are, in effect, ignoring them (as we did with Jews at the time). We've lost touch with reality.

We're also out of touch with ourselves. We're dying inside and haven't quite noticed it. We're not deeply satisfied with our lives, but instead of dealing with ourselves and finding our centers, we carry on our routines. We get two jobs so we can be surrounded by comfort (or at least would be if we ever stopped working long enough to come home). We start a savings account or invest in the money market so we can be secure (securely unhappy). We divorce and remarry because this time it will be different (though we will be unchanged ourselves). We push our kids so that where we failed they can succeed (and get bigger ulcers).

It's all emptiness, and we know it isn't working. So we plan to turn our backs on such things, as soon as we've saved enough money, found the right spouse—as soon as we sell a few more ice boxes.

But we never take the action necessary—we never get off the burning boat.

It's crazy.

It's not that we're bad people. That's one of the mysteries. How is it that perfectly nice people can let hundreds of thousands starve? How can we keep electing leaders who flirt with nuclear doom? Why don't we do more about our own hollowness?

We might expect monsters to do these things, but not decent people like ourselves. I don't understand.

Of course, in a way I do understand. Freud and Marx explain how it's done. Class interest, the unconscious, ego-defense mechanisms, and ideology allow us not to acknowledge almost anything we choose. So on some level we don't know about the starving kids—just as the Germans didn't know about the Jews. Experimental and social psychologists have also added explanations of how it's done. Selective perception, selective memory, social conformity, and the shaping of our perceptions by language—all these give us quite a free hand with reality.

So we believe whatever is in the interest of our class, whatever fits our prefabricated view of reality. If something makes us uncomfortable, we don't see it. If something might interfere with our routine, it's not true.

So Christians systematically dilute the teachings of Jesus on possessions, tobacco companies claim tobacco doesn't cause health problems, and coffee companies (faced with evidence that coffee contributes to heart disease) say the problem is with the cream people add to their coffee. We believe what we want to believe.

We can even make people disappear, as whites do with blacks. For instance, I've often heard whites say that the sports boycott of South Africa only alienates South Africans. We forget that most South Africans are black. As Huckleberry Finn said when asked if anyone was hurt in an explosion, "No'm. Killed a nigger."[2]

It's crazy, but that's how we work.

Of course, I know that we aren't clinically insane. But we behave very oddly.

I often meet people who tell me they have a hard time making ends meet, and then I figure out that they are making more than $20,000 a year. And I wonder which of us is stark raving mad.

Can't they feel how blasphemous it is to talk about their difficulty making ends meet when elsewhere people have to live on twenty-five cents a day? I know a girl in Haiti who is blind. She is blind because she didn't get enough vitamins when she was a baby. According to a doctor there, a dollar's worth of vegetables at the right time would have saved her sight.

But Americans have a hard time living on $24,580 a year (the median household income in 1983).[3] Or so they say. If they said they had a hard time *luxuriating* on $24,580, I'd think they were sane but insensitive. But they say they have a hard time *living* on $24,580. Such people have lost touch with reality—for Haiti is part of reality.

The realm of politics is equally crazy. Why else would people elect a presidential candidate who promised to balance the budget, increase military spending, and cut taxes? And how can career diplomats believe that any resistance to a capitalist government is Soviet-inspired and can only be dealt with militarily? It's crazy.

With some politicians if you explain the effects of nuclear war, they suggest that civil defense could reduce deaths in the West to a hundred million. And I once heard a politician argue that it's not forty thousand poor kids who die each day but thirty thousand. They do not seem to realize that even if they are right, what they are saying is irrelevant, obscene, and quite mad.

And then there's war. Wars are being fought in Nicaragua, Lebanon, the Ogaden region of Ethiopia and Somalia, Iraq and Iran, Afghanistan, El Salvador, Namibia, and Guatemala. People are being killed by the thousands.

But I forgot. War is not crazy—it's an instrument of state. Wars are sane.

Think about that sometime.

Maintaining this cuckoo land takes the whole array of devices explained by Freud, Marx, and the others. We tend to think that knowing is something technical: either we have the information or we don't. We imagine our eyes are like television cameras, faithfully recording whatever they look at. We suppose our minds are like computers, carefully calculating which arguments are valid. But our internal television cameras and computers have all kinds of special shunting devices and dream laboratories. To put it another way, we only acknowledge what our hearts allow us to acknowledge. If something is contrary to our self-interest, or rather to our imagined self-interest, we don't acknowledge it. So we don't know about the children starving because that would force us to change our way of life.

But at a deeper level we are not merely crazy. It is not merely a psychological matter; it is also a moral and spiritual matter. We are wicked as well as crazy. The core of sin is acting selfishly, and what Freud and Marx showed is that selfishness invades even what we know.

I do not mean that the average person is actively wicked, out killing children or cheating the poor. We are perfectly good people—wearing blinders so we won't know the ship is burning. In fact, our refusal to face up to the ship's burning is a tribute to our sensitivity. We couldn't carry on with our routine if we had absorbed the fact that people were being tortured and kids were dying. So to preserve our sense of morality, we pretend they aren't.

Of course, we could preserve our morality, as well as our sense of it, if we would face the facts. That way we could also preserve our sanity.

It is a problem of the heart. Not that we're nasty, vicious, and evil. But neither are we tenderhearted, generous, and eager to serve. If, then, the problem is a moral and spiritual one, it must be dealt with on that level. It cannot be dealt with adequately on the level of informing people about the world situation. (The information available is already extensive and reasonably adequate.) Nor can the problem be dealt with by psychotherapy. The problem is even deeper than that: What we need is a change of heart. We need to become tenderhearted so that we can feel the suffering.

What we need is to repent.

3. A Change of Heart

"Repent, for the kingdom of heaven is at hand" (Matt. 4:17). Jesus came into a world much like ours. The poverty and social structure in Palestine were comparable to the Third World today: a tiny ruling elite, a small middle class, and a vast group of poor people. And Rome was comparable to the United States and the Soviet Union: it was equally wealthy, equally oppressive, and equally willing to intervene brutally in the affairs of other nations.

And what did Jesus do in this situation? He didn't lead a guerrilla army or even organize the poor. What Jesus did was go around telling stories and proclaiming, "Repent, for the kingdom of heaven is at hand." His first concern was that people have a change of heart.

Now that doesn't necessarily mean it's wrong for followers of Jesus to join a guerrilla army or organize the poor. But we can't let such things become so important to us that we forget about repentance: Basic human change is crucial.

One of Jesus' main ways of calling people to repentance was telling stories: "The kingdom of heaven is like a merchant in search of fine pearls, who on finding one pearl of great price, went and sold all that he had and bought it" (Matt. 13:45–46). Our lives are devoted to things like success, comfort, sex, security, and pleasure. Deep down we know these things aren't what we're looking for, so sometimes we choose something a little better. Finally, we find what really counts, and we abandon them all.

What is it that is so worthwhile that we would trade everything else for it? Jesus tells us that love of God and of others is that important. Or, to use the phrase from the King James version, "on these hang all the law and the prophets" (Matt. 22:40). Other things are distractions.

Jesus' message is simple: There is something worth living for, and it isn't money or keeping the letter of the law. It's being with God and caring about people. Loving and serving— that's what life is about. All the rest is irrelevant.

Let me put it another way, a way I saw on a poster one time. "Since my storehouse burned down, I have a better view of the rising moon" and, I might add, of people walking by and maybe sometimes of God.

Have a change of heart and burn down your barns, for something worthwhile is in your grasp. Or to use Jesus' words, "Repent, for the kingdom of heaven is at hand."

Self-interest. That's the core of the human predicament. That's how we have made hell.

We weren't vicious—we just built ourselves a storage barn. Nothing wrong with that. We paid the builders fair and square, too—the barn is not built on the bones of the poor.

Of course, we couldn't let ourselves see the children dying; it might have distracted us from our task, from building our barn. So we blinded ourselves (with the storage barn). And kept on selling ice boxes. We didn't want to, but how else could we pay for our barn?

We didn't mean to pay with the bones of the poor.

But we did. And that self-interest is how the evil grows and grows. We aren't vicious—we just pick a pearl of not so great price and devote our energy to it. We have no time to fight for the kids or against the bomb: We have to hold down our job to pay for the barn.

But we *don't* have to pay for the barn—because we don't need a barn. That's half of Jesus' message: We don't need to take care of ourselves at all; God will do that. Guarding our self-interest, protecting our turf—we're set free from all that. We can love and serve instead. That's the pearl of great price. That's the change of heart we all need, the change of heart the world needs us to have.

That's repentance.

2. THE LOGIC OF JESUS

4. The Doorway to Life

"Can't I keep just one little barn?"
But Jesus didn't answer. It was the wrong question.

My daughter is supposed to go to bed at nine-thirty. But she often badgers me to let her stay up later. She seems to think that if I agree, staying up late will be okay. Usually, I insist that she go to bed on schedule because otherwise she's miserable the next day. But occasionally I say to her, "I don't care when you go to bed. It's not me who has a hard time getting up in the morning." I want her to get the idea that the reason she goes to bed is not to keep me happy; it's to keep her happy. It's related to her needs, not mine.

This same message is behind much of Jesus' teaching about the Old Testament. Many people see morality as rules made up rather arbitrarily by God. To their minds, rules are not designed to help meet human needs; they are designed as tests of human willingness to obey God. People have to force themselves into the shape of these rules as an exercise in loyalty.

The law happens to require things like, "Do not kill," and "Do not bear false witness" (Exod. 20:13, 16). But from the perspective of many people, it could almost require that we "run the marathon in less than three hours." Never mind that doing so is not crucial to living, never mind that the human body was never meant to run that way. What matters is that it's a good test of obedience.

But Jesus taught that the rules are not arbitrary; they are not to meet God's needs. Rather they are for us. Jesus tried to help people see what the law is about. It is about love—God's love for us, our love for God, and our love for other people. It is about taking care of each other the way we'd like to be taken care of. And that's no arbitrary time limit on a marathon run. It's the way to life.

So Jesus insisted on healing people on the Sabbath. It made the Pharisees furious, but it was the loving thing to do: "It is lawful to do good on the Sabbath" (Matt. 12:12). And if people are hungry, they can feed themselves even on the Sabbath: "The Sabbath was made for people, not people for the Sabbath" (Mark 2:27).

Nor is the way Jesus told us to live merely an arbitrary test. When he told us to turn the other cheek, for example, he was not setting up a new, unusually high hurdle to see if we could jump it. He was pointing us to the way of life.

"Can't I stay up late just this one time?"

"Can't I work on the Sabbath just once in a while?"

"Can't I commit adultery just one time?"

"Can't I keep just one little barn?"

"Can't I screw up my life just a little bit?"

We also have a tendency to reduce morality to rewards and punishments. We obey God's law so we won't get punished. In the process we reduce God to the great policeman in the sky—the guy whose red light we see flashing in our rearview mirror every time we break the law.

So when we ask, "Can I keep just one little barn?" what we really mean is "Will I go to hell if I keep just one little barn?" And "Seek first the kingdom, and all these things shall be yours as well" (Matt. 6:33) becomes a hot tip from God on investment: "For every ten dollars you put in the offering plate, God will return to you a hundred."

Of course, Jesus does talk about rewards and punishments, but they are never the heart of his message. Jesus does not mean that unless we sell our barns he's going to get us. He means that barns do not satisfy. They won't put our marriages back together or make our lives meaningful. The reason we're to get rid of our barns is so we can really live.

Perhaps Jesus talks about rewards and punishments to get people started on that way of life, hoping they'll deepen. In any case, behavior motivated by such things is superficial. An adult who doesn't have the sense to go to bed apart from a threat of punishment lacks something.

On some level, we know that morality is the way to life, but on another we suspect that morality prohibits all the fun things. And that suspicion comes out strongly when we think of our possessions, our rights, our status. Anyone critical of possessions must be ascetic, out to spoil our fun. Why else would Jesus say, "Woe to the rich"?

But Jesus also says, "If you want to enter life, keep the commandments" (Matt. 19:17). And his approach to possessions is not one of putting the good things off limits. Rather he says things like "People's lives do not consist in the abundance of their possessions" (Luke 12:15). Life does not consist in having barns.

Jesus sees the commandments as doorways to life. We can approach life asking how much we can keep for ourselves, or we can approach life asking how much we can give of ourselves. We can wonder what the limits of misbehavior are, beyond which God will zap us, or we can wonder what our limits are beyond which we can't serve efficiently. How far can we push the rules, or how far can we push ourselves?

The change from the one approach to the other is the change of direction God wants. This change is a paradigm shift, a conversion to a different world view. Jesus did not come to give us another set of rules. He was not adding "No possessions" to "No adultery," nor was he adding "Love your neighbor" to "Honor your parents." Rather he came to offer us another way to look at life. As long as we think Jesus was giving us rules, we'll never get anyplace. He was not giving us rules; he was trying to do something to our minds and hearts. Jesus is trying to awaken us to a logic of giving, a logic of superabundance. He wants us to outgrow stinginess, our grasping for things. He is telling us we never again have to figure out how to get tit for tat, an eye for an eye. We no longer need to calculate whether our turf is protected, our future secure, our rights safe. We are free to reach out.

So which will we choose? The logic of open hands or the logic of white knuckles?

Love is something if you give it way, you end up having more. It's just like a magic penny. Hold it tight, and you don't have any. Lend it, spend it, and you'll have so many, they'll roll all over the floor. So let's go dancing till the break of day, and if there's a piper we can pay 'cause love is something if you give it way, you end up having more.[1]

All the rest of life is like that, too.

"Ah, but can I keep one little barn?"

To say, "No, you can't" would be nearly as wrong as saying, "Yes, keep three." Both are white knuckled. A better answer might be, "Keep all you want," but that would be misunderstood.

So Jesus walked silently away.

Is our approach to life one of overflowing generosity? Or do we measure out our lives in coffee spoons and savings accounts? Are we looking for ways to share more, or are we trying to justify holding on to something? Are we trying to figure out how many barns we can get rid of or how many we can hold on to?

No matter what we ask, do we ask with open hands or with white knuckles?

"You mean it really doesn't matter about my keeping three barns as long as my attitude is right?"

And Jesus walked silently away.

We imagine that the Pharisees' rules would have been good if they had been about love or justice instead of about ceremonial trivia. And that certainly would have been an improvement. But the Pharisees' primary mistake was to suppose that if they didn't walk on the Sabbath, they were worshiping God. And that is not necessarily so. By deciding how many steps they could take on the Sabbath, they limited what they gave to God: I don't have to give myself to God, they said, I don't have to actually love God; not walking will do. This is the wrong logic, the logic of stinginess, of white knuckles. By the same token, if we decide how much of our income we must give away, we are also setting limits on how much we need to give away. At a certain point we will have done enough. But we can never do enough.

We can never do enough. That's one of the reasons Jesus didn't give a system of rules. If he had, he would have been setting limits beyond which we'd have no need to go. When we reached those limits, if not well before, we would become complacent and proud. We would quit before we'd reached home. That's the logic of limits: What's the least I can do and still be in good standing?

When I was in high school, I ran cross-country, and every Thursday we had time trials. If we ran too slowly, we had to run the course over again, but for those of us who took cross-country seriously, that was hardly the point. We wanted to see how fast we could run, not how long we could take without getting into trouble.

I was sometimes delighted by how fast I ran, but I still hoped I would run faster the next time. In a race you can never run fast enough, never reach a limit beyond which you needn't go. That is not a legalism that weighs you down; it is an exciting goal that pulls you forward.

That's like Jesus. He knows no limits. He wants everything. All of us. Down to the last barn.

5. Thirty Days to a Deeper Spiritual Life?

"Exactly how many barns must I give away?"
But Jesus walked silently away. It was the wrong question.

We have simple, unpoetic minds. We want to be told clearly what to do. How many thousands of dollars can we spend each year before we give the rest away? How many grams of meat can we eat before we've eaten more than our share?

We want an ethical system with general principles, extensive applications, and a list of exceptions. But no, Jesus lays on a guilt trip about turning the other cheek and not asking for our things back when someone takes them. We want an illustration, and he tells us to give to those who beg. What is the principle that his command illustrates? Or is it an exception to a principle? And why doesn't he give us criteria for worthy causes to give to?

We live in a scientific age. We'd like principles for living as precise as the laws of physics: $E=mc^2$ and all that. But Jesus spoke in pictures and gave us aphorisms that he rarely expanded.

At least we'd like principles as clear as legislation: For all the law's vagueness a body of interpretation has grown up around it, and there are courts to decide its proper application. But Jesus gave us principles so vast they confound us and specifics so pungent we know he can't have meant them literally.

We want exact formulae, statistical tables, precise criteria, but that was not Jesus' style. He dropped verbal bombs.

Even our art is utilitarian and decorative (not to mention our ethics). To relax, we may read about hobbits, but only because

we think they're unreal. Yet Jesus left us with parables and figures of speech, questions and pithy sayings, hyperbole and mystery, children and rude remarks, the birds of the air and . . . silence.
With our literal minds, how are we supposed to understand Jesus?

"Exactly how many barns must I give away?"

"Can I have one pair of wool pants, or must I wear washable clothes all the time?"

"How many steps may I take on the sabbath?"

Jesus doesn't gave us thirty easy lessons to the deeper spiritual life. (Anyone who does is a fraud.) Life isn't like that. Life is too complex, too full of paradox. It needs to be understood on many different levels. Above all it needs to be seen before it can be said. We need to participate actively to understand anything about life—memorizing a list of rules won't do.

So Jesus is not giving us a list of rules. He is trying to show us life. He gives us parables we have to wrestle with. When we ask about greatness, he sits a child on his lap. He says things like, "If someone grabs your coat, offer him your shirt as well." If we try to see the world that way, everything wobbles and seems upside-down.

Jesus is trying to shake our perception of things so that we'll gain a new vision of reality. He wants us to experience a paradigm shift. As we struggle to understand what he is saying, we are wrenched partly free of the limited way we saw it before; we get a little peek of a deeper view. If he gave us twelve rules we could memorize, even twelve very good ones, we would be frozen at whatever level we understood them. Jesus instead wants to nudge us and shock us onto the next level. He wants us to experience a whole series of paradigm shifts. He paints us a picture hoping that we'll be drawn into it.

And we complain that the picture isn't precise enough! *Life*

Made Simple (and false) is what we wish the Gospels were called.

"But how many grams of protein. . . ."
Why not ask instead, "How do I get home from here?"

When I was in grade school, we had a Sunday school lesson about Samuel's choosing one of Jesse's sons to be king. He wanted to pick the oldest, the tallest, the strongest. But God told him, "The Lord does not see as human beings see. They look on the outward appearance, but the Lord looks on the heart" (1 Sam. 16:7). For months after that I went around pretending I could see right through people to their true selves. I imagined I wasn't impressed by rank or muscle or looks or popularity. I saw only the real world, not how it looked.

I guess I didn't fully understand the story. If I had, I wouldn't have cast myself as Superman (not even with x-ray vision of a spiritual sort). But I had the general idea. God wants us to look right through strength and money and such. God wants us to see the real world, not reflections in distorting mirrors.

God wants us to have a new vision.
"Yes, but doesn't our vision have to tell us exactly how many barns to keep?"

Human beings desire clear answers. We want to be certain what is right. We want to know for sure what job to take, what church to join, what school to attend. We want to avoid ambiguity at all costs. So people who promise answers get large followings. And ideologies have many true believers. Most of us, though to varying degrees, want infallible rule books, ouija boards, reliable horoscopes, or a clear calling from the Lord.

This desire for clarity is the reason for TV religion, Jim Jones, orthodox Marxism, inflexible campaigns both for and against abortion, fundamentalism, and, I suppose, radical Christianity. Each of them provides a system full of answers.

When I first came across Bill Gothard's seminars on basic

youth conflicts, I was impressed by the way he gave specific steps for dealing with problems. I was appalled by the actual steps he gave, but I thought that what we needed was equally specific answers, but answers that reflected Jesus' teaching. So I started thinking of seminars on radical discipleship.

But Jesus refuses to feed such adolescent fantasies. He gave the Sermon on the Mount and told parables that even the disciples didn't understand. He wants to jar us out of all our systems.

"But I still don't know how many . . ."

You have to get down to specifics sometime. Maybe I don't need to know how many grams of protein is my share, but I do need to know whether I should eat meat or be a vegetarian. I need to know how to apply the saying about offering my shirt to someone who seizes my coat: If someone demands my money at knife point, am I obliged to offer my watch as well? Does getting rid of my barns include selling my car?

Not only does Jesus fail to offer thirty steps to the deeper spiritual life, he doesn't even give much concrete, pragmatic guidance. What he does on the practical level is merely point us in a direction. He tells us which way is home. He sets us on the road.

We think we need to know all the details before we can set out on a journey. But Jesus' idea was for us to set out. Then we could follow the signs, we could get better maps as we went along, we could ask advice from wise guides.

6. Backwardness Training

"But I still don't know how many barns I can keep."

What Jesus is telling us is that we have it all backwards. The direction we're headed does not lead home. What we need to do is to turn completely around and go the opposite way.

We think the thing to do is to get a job with a higher salary so we can buy a bigger house. But Jesus is telling us that we're being silly (or worse). Possessions have nothing to do with it, or rather they get in the way. They distract us.

We worry about who is greater than us, and in response Jesus takes a child on his lap. That, of course, prompts us to do a prolonged study on which aspect of childhood Jesus wants us to emulate, and in the process we miss his point. He's saying, "You've got it all backwards again. Don't try to be like a member of the Sanhedrin or of Herod's court. Try to be like this kid, who isn't at all important. Importance is unimportant, or worse."

In Jesus' time, the Jews were fiercely independent, but Israel had been occupied by pagan Romans. The Jews hated the occupying army and searched for ways to retaliate (much as they might today if the Palestine Liberation Organization ruled them). But what does Jesus tell them? If an occupying soldier makes you carry his pack for a mile, say to him: "May I carry it another mile for you, sir?" In other words, you've got it all backwards. Again.

"You mean fretting about how many barns I can keep is all backwards? But I like my barns. Can't I keep just one?"

"I know I'm going the wrong way, but can't I go just a little further?"

"All the way to hell, if that's where you want to go."

Jesus specializes in reversing standard wisdom, in contradicting our instincts. "Love your enemies. Do good to those who hate you. Bless those who curse you. If someone takes your things, don't ask for them back."

It's as if Jesus made a list of the things we value, the things that motivate us, and stood them on their heads. "You pursue money, lots of food, laughter, respectability, good looks, intelligence, strength, health, good clothes, getting even, but I tell you, you'd be better off poor, hungry, crying, hated, ugly, dumb, weak, sick, shabby, and trodden on." In fact, that's not a bad paraphrase of Luke's version of the Beatitudes.

Or consider this paraphrase: You think it's good to be rich? Well, you're wrong. Riches are a mess. It's you poor who are fortunate. You think it's good to be well fed now? You're wrong. You'd be better off hungry. You think you should pursue laughter? That's a mistake. Those who weep are ahead. You want to be respected and admired by everyone in sight? Well you've got it upside down. Respect is a problem. You're fortunate if people despise you and won't even let you into their churches and clubs (see Luke 6:20–26).

Jesus isn't giving us a list of rules: You must be poor, crying, sickly, stupid, and ugly. He's telling us we're going the wrong way. We're trying to acquire possessions when we should be trying to disentangle ourselves from them. We're trying to live a life free of sorrows when instead we should be doing what needs to be done, which won't be easy. We go to fanatical ends to preserve our health, but if we do what's right someone will break both our legs anyway. We take every opportunity to show how smart we are, but we are ruined because we don't really believe that dumb people are as important as we are. If we're beautiful, we parade it, not realizing we are going the wrong way and have become proud of an irrelevant bauble.

Which direction are you going? What's your vision of life? Those are Jesus' questions.

"Okay. I'll carry the pack a second mile. But let me tell you, when I've carried it 10,560 feet, I'm going to throw it on the ground."

"You mean I should cry at least once a day?"

"You mean I can't have any barns at all?"

And Jesus walked silently away.

One time I went to the bank with a friend to help him get a mortgage on a house. They asked him what assets he had, and he said he had a couple thousand dollars in a no-interest loan to Koinonia. The bank officer asked, literally, "A couple thousand dollars in a what?" The bank officer had never heard of a no-interest loan.

Now I don't know for sure whether we should get mortgages on houses, but I'm confident my friend was on the right track. He was doing something backwards enough that a bank officer had trouble understanding it. That's an encouraging sign.

Some churches, in order to show what good work they do, advertise the impressive people they've helped. They parade converted millionaires, beauty queens, Supreme Court justices, athletes, movie stars, and mayors. They think that these "success" stories authenticate their message. Those churches still have it backwards.

But once in a while you find churches that realize the world has been turned upside down. They serve prostitutes, criminals, drug addicts, the unemployed, illegal aliens, retarded people—outcasts, not people of rank. This is an encouraging sign—these churches are going in the right direction.

I don't know how much money we should spend, but if people are impressed by how much we spend, then we're almost surely going the wrong way. And if the money you live on is little enough that people can't believe it when they hear it, then you are probably going the right direction. You may not have reached the magic level where the amount you spend is all right (in fact, you can't have since there is no such number), but you've started.

"Am I on the way if I've only got one barn left?"
And Jesus walked silently away.

Those who study missions tell a story about India. There many of the converts to Christianity are from the lowest rung of society. They are not from the lowest caste. They are below that—they are outcasts. They are the garbage collectors, the people who pick up the manure, the ones who clean the toilets. In time the word *Christian* came to mean *toilet cleaner*, or so the story goes.

A missionary was working with a Brahmin, an aristocratic Indian. The missionary gave a critique of Hinduism and offered arguments for Christianity. Finally he felt the person was ready, so he asked him whether he wanted to become a Christian. The Brahmin turned on his heel and left. Later the missionary realized the problem. He had asked the Brahmin whether he wanted to become a toilet cleaner, a person below caste.

That story is usually told to show that Christianity shouldn't become totally associated with any low-status group, because of possible confusion. The Brahmin was angered because he didn't understand the question; he mistakenly thought he was being asked to be a toilet cleaner.

But I wonder. I wonder if maybe he did understand. Maybe he understood exactly. To become a Christian is to turn everything upside down, and that, especially for a Brahmin, means becoming a toilet cleaner; but he, like the rich, young ruler, wasn't about to do that.

God wants us to see life backwards, upside down, and inside out.

"How much of my wealth can I give away?"
Jesus said, "Blessed. . . .

7. Eating Your Cake and Having It Too

"Can I keep my barn as long as I don't care about it?"

"Can I repent without changing?"

The trouble is, we want to have it both ways. We want to live in the upside-down kingdom while staying right side up. We want to stand on our heads while keeping our feet solidly on the ground.

We can understand what Jesus is saying, but we don't want to accept the consequences. (That is, we don't understand what Jesus is saying.)

We want to recognize the triviality of material possessions. While keeping them.

We want to reject fame and power. While being famous and powerful.

We want our treasure to be in heaven. But we'll keep our stocks and bonds, thank you very much.

We know looks and intelligence are unimportant. But we're sure glad when our kids are smart and handsome.

"Can I head home without changing my course?"

"Can I lead a full life while drinking poison?"

So Jesus tells us we must choose. It's either/or, not both/and. Christians can't have a foot in both camps—we're either hot or cold, not lukewarm. No fence-sitting.

"No one can serve two masters; for either you will hate the one and love the other, or you will be devoted to one and despise the other. You cannot serve God and mammon" (Matt. 6:24).

Would you say you despise your barn? Or are you devoted to it, just a little? Would you mind if it burned? If so, Jesus says you despise God. He wants us to choose.

"How about if I serve God but keep just one or two barns?"

God, of course, is what really counts to church members. Though we keep just a little treasure in the bank.

That's the way we think, but Jesus makes himself hoarse saying things like, "Do not lay up for yourselves treasures on earth. For where your treasure is, there will your heart be also" (Matt. 6:19, 21). He never says things like, "Your main treasure should be in heaven with not too much on earth."

Jesus thinks in dichotomies. "I desire mercy, not sacrifice" (Matt. 9:13; 12:7). "I have not come to bring peace, but a sword" (Matt. 10:34). "Those who find their lives will lose them" (Matt. 10:39). "Those who are not with me are against me, and they who do not gather with me scatter" (Matt. 12:30, but see Luke 9:50). "Whoever would be first among you must be your slave, even as the Son of man came not to be served but to serve" (Matt. 20:27–28). "Those who exalt themselves will be humbled" (Matt. 23:12).

With Jesus, it's all or nothing. But as for those of us who sit in darkness, we may have seen a great light, but we intend to live in the dusk.

"Can I keep my barn as long as I don't care about it?"
"If you don't care about it, why do you care whether you can keep it?"

8. Hedonistic Paradox

"Can't I hold on to just a little bit of what I have?"

Jesus tells us that we can, after all, eat our cake and have it too. But not by holding on to just a little bit of it. That will leave us poor. Paradoxically, the way to have our cake is to give it up.

"If any of you would come after me, deny yourself and take up your cross and follow me. For any of you who would save your life will lose it, and whoever of you loses your life for my sake will find it. For what will it profit you if you gain the whole world and lose your soul? Or what would you give in return for your life?" (Matt. 16: 24–26).

Jesus' way is a different sort of life. In it we don't have to fight to make sure we get ours. In fact, it is when we turn our back on getting ours that we finally do get it. Until then life is a perpetual cat fight, even if you get your way. (To change the image, the trouble with a rat race is that even if you win you are still a rat.)

The way kids can ruin good times grubbing for their own way is especially clear. (They aren't sophisticated enough to hide it.) I swear I've seen kids enraged over the TV program they're watching, enraged not because they didn't like the program (it might even have been the one that they would have chosen), but because they didn't get to choose it themselves. And I've seen my kids simultaneously miserable because each thought the other had a bigger serving of ice cream.

And I do the same sort of thing, only I'm more sophisticated. The point is that we have to get beyond the stage of protecting our rights and measuring ourselves against what others have, or we can't enjoy what we do have. We all keep asking ourselves questions like, "What if someone grabs some of my turf? What plans can I make ahead of time to prevent it?" But Jesus wants us to get beyond this kind of scheming. He wants our reaction to be, "Do you want some of my turf? Here, take it."

Sometimes it's called the hedonistic paradox: If you pursue pleasure, you won't find it. When it's in your grasp, it turns out not to be pleasurable—it turns to ashes in your mouth. Those pursuing something else, especially something deeper, are the ones who find pleasure and happiness. (Though perhaps on a cross or in a prison cell.)

Those not worried about fulfillment are the ones who enjoy the sunset and see the birds of the air. Those seeking fulfillment need cocaine to make the sunset more intense. It is the Mother Teresas who are content, who will die happy—not the Hugh Heffners.

Or so Jesus tells us.

"If I sell my barn, how much will I get back?"
And Jesus walked silently away.

What appears to be in our self-interest isn't always. In fact, it rarely is. That's a lot of Jesus' message to us. We can either live life to the hilt, getting ourselves crucified in the process, or we can live a miserly, miserable existence, perhaps surrounded by wealth and power, which we use ourselves up protecting.

The question Jesus raises is about ultimate concern. We're concerned about things like pleasure and happiness, food and clothing, wealth and power. But Jesus tells us that these things are not of ultimate concern. It's when we do find things that are of ultimate concern that other things find their rightful place and life becomes worth living.

But human beings are inclined to be distracted by shiny baubles and imitation pearls. The absence of ultimate concern leaves a huge void, and we try to stuff it full with other things that aren't ultimate: pleasure, happiness, sex, gadgets, status, our kids, whatever. But we're trying to fill the emptiness with empty things, and we find only more emptiness.

The key to filling the emptiness is to give up ourselves—our rights, our possessions, our plans. When we give ourselves away, we also give our emptiness away. And we are filled, generously: "Give, and it will be given to you; good measure, pressed down, shaken together, running over, will be put into your lap" (Luke 6:38).

"How many barns shall I give away?"

"It all depends how full a life you want to live."

3. THE BIBLE AND POSSESSIONS: A LOOK AT SOME TEXTS

9. Obscenity

One time I was leaving Manila, and I realized I had a pocketful of change. Since you can't exchange small coins, I decided to buy lunch and a coke at an outdoor stand. I didn't really need to eat because I knew I'd be fed on the plane, but I couldn't think what else to do with the change.

As I was eating, I noticed a little girl sorting through trash cans. I wondered idly what she was after but didn't give it much thought—I sometimes go through trash cans myself to get a newspaper. Then I saw that the little girl was collecting paper cups. She had hundreds of paper cups.

I assume that collecting paper cups was not a hobby of hers. (Only the wealthy indulge in such whimsy.) I assume she sold them. If she was lucky, she might have gotten twenty-five cents for a day's collecting. About then she started eyeing me, and I realized her look was not idle, the way mine had been: She wanted my cup.

That was embarrassing. Not because I was caught drinking something sugary, artificial, and from the West. (Ah, the sensitive consciences of the comfortable.) The problem was that I hadn't been able to think what else to do with my change. And the drink I didn't need had cost as much as the little girl was likely to earn all day. Not to mention the food. So I drank my coke as quickly as I could and handed her the empty cup. She gave me a big grin.

Which didn't exactly make my day: She reminded me too much of my own daughter. Except my daughter's eyes are blue, and her hair is blond, and her skin is white.

And she doesn't go through trash cans.

In the presence of grinding poverty, wealth is obscene.
It is obscene that we buy cokes whenever we want while

many Third World babies can't get enough milk. It is obscene that our toolsheds are nicer than many Third World homes. (I wonder how many poor people could live in our two-car garages?) It is obscene that we feed our pets better than many Third World parents feed their kids. (We also get our pets better health care.) It is obscene that we can afford cigarettes to kill ourselves while many Third World people can't afford beans to stay alive. It is obscene that I couldn't think of anything else to do with my change.

And the extremely wealthy are not the only ones who commit these obscenities. In the West, even quite ordinary people (like me) do it all the time. Even quite ordinary Westerners are wealthy by Third World standards.

Manila has some of the most luxurious hotels in the world. One of them has a mammoth swimming pool, surrounded by high walls and palm trees. Beside it is a lovely garden with fountains. In the water along the shallow side of the pool are bar stools, with a counter in front of them. The pavement beside the pool is sunken so that the bartender is at eye level with the patrons. There the elite, at ease, can sip their whiskey sours, with their bodies half under the cool water—after all, it gets hot in Manila.

Of course, it also gets hot a couple of miles away in Tondo, one of the world's awful slums.

As Amos said:

Woe to those who are at ease in Zion [Manila],
　　to those who feel secure on the mountain of Samaria [Baguio],
　　the notable people of this important nation.
Woe to those who lie on beds of ivory
　　and stretch themselves on their couches [or underwater bar stools]
　　and eat lamb and veal;
Who sing idle songs to the sound of the guitar,
　　and like David invent new musical instruments for themselves;
Who drink wine from bowls [or whiskey sours from specially shaped
　　glasses]

and anoint themselves with [cologne],
but are not grieved over the ruin of Joseph [Tondo]!
Therefore they shall now be the first of those to go into exile [cap-
    tured by the guerrillas],
and the revelry of those who stretch themselves [on underwater
    bar stools] shall end. (Amos 6:1, 4–7)

I see nothing in itself wrong with feeding cats tuna fish or even with having luxurious swimming pools. The problem is Tondo. David's making new musical instruments was not wrong, but you don't do such things while Tondo or Joseph is suffering. While forty thousand kids are starving each day, cats eating tuna fish present a dilemma. And while thousands in Tondo have no way of making a decent living, luxurious hotels are not even a dilemma.

Jesus sums it up better than I can. Remember the passage about Lazarus and Dives?

There was an average American who drove a Volkswagen and ate all he wanted every day. And in Colombia lay a little boy who would have been happy with the American's scraps. The little boy died of starvation and was carried by angels to Abraham's lap. The American also died, only he went to hell. In torment, he looked up and saw Abraham holding the boy. And the rich man called, "Abraham, have mercy on me and send the boy to me with a drink, for I am in agony in this fire." Abraham replied, "You in your lifetime received your good things while the boy received bad things, but now he is comforted and you are in agony." Then the American asked Abraham to send the boy to American churches so that not all church members would go to hell. But Abraham said, "They have Moses and Paul; let them hear them." "No," said the American, "if someone goes to them from the dead, they will repent." Abraham said to him, "If they do not hear Moses and Paul, neither will they be convinced if someone rose from the dead." (Luke 16:19–31)

One of the notable things about this passage is that it does not suggest that the rich man got his wealth by wrong means. It does not suggest he was an oppressor. It does not even suggest that he had too many possessions or that he ate too well. It merely tells what will happen to those who are at ease and indifferent to the suffering of others.

Not sharing is obscene.

Interestingly, in the Old Testament being at ease is often treated as a bad thing. So Isaiah says,

> Rise up, you women who are at ease, hear my voice;
>   you complacent daughters, give ear to my speech.
> In a little more than a year
>   you will shudder, you complacent women;
>   for the vintage will fail,
>   the fruit harvest will not come.
> Tremble, you women who are at ease,
>   shudder you complacent ones. (Isa. 32:9–11)

And Job says, "In the thought of one who is at ease, there is contempt for misfortune" (Job 12:5). Something about the sleek complacency of people who are at ease is offensive to God.[1]

As Ezekiel says, "Behold, this was the guilt of your sister Sodom: she and her daughters had pride, surfeit of food, and prosperous ease, but did not aid the poor and needy" (Ezek. 16:14). Sodom's surfeit of food and her prosperous ease were not wrong in themselves, but as long as some people were poor and needy, her money should have been spent on them.

It's a question of priorities.

10. On Not Wasting Your Life

Wasting your life is a terrible thing. I suppose it's better than damaging the lives of others, but not much. (It's better the way suicide is better than murder.)

Yet wasting our lives is exactly what most of us do. We spend our time doing things that don't matter. Not that we do vicious things, only pointless ones (though people with empty lives often turn vicious).

So we sell cosmetics or try to get shirts whiter. We do crossword puzzles or organize Tupperware parties. Not to mention going to spectator sports and reading trashy books. And selling ice boxes.

These things are not necessarily wrong, but if our time is spent predominately on such trivia, then our lives are trivial. We are wasting them. Which is a terrible thing—especially when the deck is burning.

> Why do you spend your money for that which
> is not bread,
> and your labor for that which does not satisfy? (Isa. 55:2)

It's a question of priorities. What is important enough to deserve spending our time on? Jesus had a lot to say to that question, but before looking at his teaching, let's look at the Old Testament background of his teaching.

The Ten Commandments themselves give implicit teaching on priorities. The first commandment, "You shall have no other God before me" (Exod. 20:3), implies that God is the first priority. And the last commandment, "You shall not covet" (Exod. 20:17), deals with the pursuit of possessions. The first may seem to deal only with which temple to attend, so to speak, and the last only with not pursuing your *neighbor's* possessions. But I think they reach deeper than that: they set priorities.

The priority of God is established not only by what the commandments say but also by their structure. The first commandment is *first* and is therefore in the place of greatest prominence. Furthermore, the introduction to the commandments, as well as all three of the initial commandments, are about God:

> I am the Lord your God, who brought you out of the land of Egypt, out of the house of bondage. You shall have no other Gods before me. You shall not make for yourself a graven image. . . . You shall not take the name of the Lord your God in vain. (Exod. 20:2–4, 7)

You cannot easily read these verses without seeing that God is what counts—God is the first priority. The Lord God is not like the Canaanite gods with whom the god of war, say, could be played off against the goddess of fertility. But as Deuteronomy says, "The Lord is God in heaven above and on the earth beneath; there is no other" (4:39).

The tenth commandment may also be given a place of prominence by its position: The first and last items in a list are the ones most likely to be remembered. In any case, coveting was seen as an important enough problem to be treated in the commandments themselves. Greed (giving too much priority to possessions) was considered a serious matter.

Among the Old Testament books, Psalms and Proverbs are the ones that discuss priorities most clearly. Psalms 19 and 119 make explicit the low priority of possessions. Much of Psalm 19 and all of 119 are devoted to praising the law. The path God intended for us is far better than any other, including wealth:

> The ordinances of the Lord are true
>   and righteous altogether.
> More to be desired are they than gold,
>   even much fine gold;
> Sweeter also than honey
>   and drippings of the honeycomb. (Ps. 19:9–10)

Psalm 119 says things like, "The law of your mouth is better to me than thousands of pieces of gold and silver" (v. 72), "The Lord is my portion" (v. 57), and "I love your commandments above gold, above fine gold" (v. 127).

Proverbs has a collection of similar sayings, but in them it is wisdom (not the law) that is to be pursued:

> Take my instruction instead of silver
>   and knowledge rather than choice gold;
> for wisdom is better than jewels. (8:10)

Wisdom is preeminent, but in Proverbs a lot of things, human things, are seen as more important than wealth:

> Better is a little with fear of the Lord
>   than great treasure and trouble with it.
> Better is a dinner of herbs where love is
>   than a fatted ox and hatred with it. (15: 16–17)

> It is better to be of lowly spirit with the poor
>   than to divide the spoil with the proud. (16:19)

> Better is a poor person with integrity
>   than a rich person with perverse ways. (28:6)

The picture of the good life that emerges from Proverbs (not just these verses) is that of a hard-working family that love each other and are at peace. Wisdom, justice, and godliness are to be pursued rather than wealth and power, for being of humble means is no tragedy, and being wealthy is no great gain. This is a human and sensible view of the world, in sharp contrast to the usual fare in today's media.

Notice that these sayings do not beat people over the head for having wrong priorities. Rather they tell us that wealth is a dead-end. The law, the fear of the Lord, wisdom—these are the doorways to life. These have ultimate value, and we are wasting ourselves if we pursue anything else.

The Prophets also sometimes deal with the priority of possessions. (Haggai 1:1–11 does, and so, to a lesser extent, do Jeremiah 9:23–24, 22:13–19, and Micah 3:9–13.) But usually the

Prophets discuss the injustice of the wealthy rather than their perverse priorities. However, my favorite statement about the emptiness of things and the fullness of God's way is from the Prophets.

> Ho, everyone who thirsts,
>   come to the waters;
> And you who have no money,
>   come, buy and eat!
> Come, buy wine and milk
>   without money and without price.
> Why do you spend your money for that which is not bread,
>   and your labor for that which does not satisfy?
> Hearken diligently to me, and eat what is good,
>   and delight yourself in fatness. (Isa. 55:1-2)

The way of the Lord may not be the way of financial wealth, but neither is it one of grim asceticism. God's way is one of joy and fullness. It is the way not to waste yourself.

Jesus continues the Old Testament teaching that pursuit of possessions should take low priority. But he develops it his own way. He ups the ante. Saying that a dinner of herbs with love is better than a fatted ox sets priorities, but it also opens the door to trying to have both. In fact, it almost implies that the ideal is a fatted ox with love. We, of course, are delighted by this; we are firm believers that we can have both. (See chapter 6.)

But Jesus will have none of it. We must choose:

> No one can serve two masters; for either he will hate the one and love the other, or he will be devoted to the one and despise the other. You cannot serve God and mammon. (Matt. 6:24)

Of course, serving mammon is one sin nobody commits. We all know other people who serve mammon, but none of us does— a phenomenon that makes it strange that Jesus warns against it (or is the strangeness how little we know about ourselves?). No matter how much of our strength is spent earning money, no matter how much of our energy goes into maintaining our house, no matter how many thousands we salt away, no matter if we are drowning in a sea of things, we insist we're not serving mammon.

The problem here is that serving is a matter of attitude. Serving mammon does not mean having possessions; it means being enslaved to them. We are dealing with attitudes, and attitudes are easier to hide than possessions. We can hide attitudes even from ourselves (or perhaps I should say we can hide them especially from ourselves). As a result, when we hear Jesus' teaching on wealth, we are able to twist it until we justify whatever we are doing. We may own lots of things, but we do not serve them.

Or so we say.

We need greater honesty and self-awareness. Jesus' teaching here is about attitudes, thus forcing us into self-examination. But Jesus gives no legalistic criteria, no magic tests to tell whether we're serving money. To find our way in the life Jesus intended for us, we have to get to know ourselves. And for modern people that may not be easy.

One way to get to know ourselves better is to ask ourselves who our master is. Implied in Jesus' teaching here is that all of us have some master. We tend to imagine that we're free and independent agents who do what we please. But aren't we all servants of someone or something? The only question is *whom* or *what* we serve. And whether we know it.

My observation is that few people actually have God as master. I don't think I have, except maybe by fits and starts. (At the moment, getting this book written is my master.) And what Jesus seems to be saying is that if God is not our master, then our job, our house, our status, the kids, the lottery—*something*—is. And the most likely candidate is possessions.

Now Jesus never says outright that the most likely candidate is possessions. But possessions are what he keeps returning to. Jesus says more about possessions than about anything else. In Luke nearly 20 percent of what Jesus says is about possessions.[1]

No other topic even comes close. Sex, for example, is certainly a very important topic, but Jesus speaks about it only a few times. However, he returns to possessions again and again.

In the Old Testament, idolatry is denounced more than anything else (with injustice a close second). In the New Testament, the warnings are not against worshiping Baal but against worshiping mammon. The most likely form of idolatry today is materialism (Paul explicitly equates the two in Ephesians 5:5 and Colossians 3:5), and I would suppose that people today worship money every bit as often as the Israelites did Baal.

If Jesus sees possessions as that big a threat, why don't we? How do we persuade ourselves that our attitudes toward possessions are all right?

> Why do you spend your money for that which is not bread,
> and your labor for that which does not satisfy? (Isa. 55:2)

Since the question of priorities is one of attitude, we sometimes think that our behavior is irrelevant. We kid ourselves into thinking that the amount we own or the amount we have saved doesn't matter as long as our attitude is right. But behavior and attitudes are integrally connected. Our priorities shape what we do.

In fact, one of the best guides to our priorities is our budget. Certainly, our budget is a better guide than what we *say* is important to us. Consider budgets on a national level. If a nation decides to spend more on arms and less on the poor, then you know that its priorities are wrong. And what that country says its priorities are is irrelevant.

The same is true of churches. Examine a church's budget to see how much it spends on pastoral care, how much on evangelism, how much on the poor, and how much on its buildings. That information will tell you what really matters in that church.

And the same is true on a personal level. Forty thousand kids dying each day because they are poor should have some effect on how we spend our money. Yet Americans probably spend more on candy than American Christians give to the Third World.[2] We spend three times as much on cigarettes as on foreign economic aid and six times as much on alcohol.[3] Which makes it perfectly clear that the average person's attitude toward money is not appropriate. How can we say our attitude is fine when little kids are starving and in addition to our color television we buy a color Polaroid camera and better earphones for our stereo?

I know that few who read this book are wealthy. But compared to much of the world, the average American has unimaginable wealth. In 1979 America had a per capita gross national product of $9,590. Meanwhile thirty-six countries with a combined population of two billion people had per capita gross national products of less than $300.[4] Remember that right now over half a billion people are hungry, and you will understand my point.

Did you ever wonder why old houses have so few closets? It's mostly because people then didn't have so many things.

Remember how many closets you have. They are for storing things you aren't using. In my house, we have six closets, and we'd like to add a coat closet. In addition to our six closets, we also have a basement. And a shed. And a pantry. All pretty full.

What is your attitude toward possessions if your closets are bursting with things you don't use while kids starve by the thousands?

Why do you spend your labor for that which does not satisfy?

We are in fact prisoners of our possessions. To maintain our possessions, we have to keep our jobs. We have lost our freedom.

Sometimes, our bondage is pretty obvious. If we have sizeable mortgages, car payments, refrigerator payments, and payments on new roofs, we may realize that we're prisoners. We're stuck at our job until our debts are paid.

But more often our imprisonment is hidden. We don't have a lot of debts; just a lot of needs. We are prisoners of these needs. We *need* a decent car (or is it two?). We *need* a house big enough for each child to have his or her own room. (No one in the history of the world has believed such a thing before now, though it seems obvious to me and almost all other Americans.) I *need* a stereo; other people need a color television. And clothes—it is incredible how many clothes we need. And money to go see the Eagles beat the Cowboys. Not to mention music lessons, bicycles, and allowances for the kids.

What master do we serve in this prison?

This is no idle question: We are unable to do the things that matter because we have to hold down our job to meet our needs. We can't take a job with Bread for the World because they don't pay enough. We hate to keep being engineers for a company that may use our work in missiles, but no one else pays well enough. In most houses no one can do volunteer work against torture because the adults have to work full time to meet economic needs.

I believe that this economic control is the central control device of our civilization. We can't say no to the insane wickedness of our world; we can't afford to. But if we could get free of some of those "needs," large numbers of us could quit our jobs and challenge the arms race (or whatever). Our kids might not get music lessons, as important as they are, but they'd be less likely to get killed in a nuclear holocaust. And that's kind of important, too.

Why do you spend your labor for that which does not satisfy?

Basic changes of this sort are what Jesus meant by repentance and rebirth. We need a change of heart. It goes deeper than accepting certain rules; it is a reversal of priorities.

But notice that this change of heart is not simply a refusal to serve mammon—that by itself would leave emptiness. It also requires finding a new master: God. As we come to see that possessions aren't worth devoting our lives to, we need to find something that is. Otherwise, we'll find ourselves like the writer of Ecclesiastes who makes excellent statements about the futility of possessions—and of everything else. If we stop there, we dry up or become bitter. Or we accept an even worse master. (Remember the story of the evil spirit who was cast out of a person but returned later because the person remained empty—Matt. 12:43–45.)

Jesus is not just negative about possessions—he points us toward real life as well. When a man asks Jesus (Luke 12:13–15) to help him get more of the family inheritance, Jesus refuses. (The teacher who said we shouldn't ask for goods back when someone takes them could hardly say anything else.) The reason he gives for refusing is that life does not consist in the abundance of possessions. Life is *more* than food, and the body is *more* than clothing (Luke 12:15, 23).

Then there is Jesus' delightful statement, one of my favorite in the Bible: "Fear not, little flock, for it is your Father's good pleasure to give you the kingdom" (Luke 12:32). A gentler statement I can hardly imagine. It's really a promise—God is a far kinder master than possessions.

And yet this gentle promise is immediately followed by the thunderous command: "Sell your possessions" (Luke 12:33). But I suggest that the command is equally gentle; the thunder is in our own ears because we are still devoted to our possessions. Selling our possessions is the way to life, to the gentle kingdom. That is the way not to waste our lives. And as we get our priorities straight, the command to sell our possessions will sound less thunderous.

> Ho, everyone who thirsts,
>   come to the waters;
> And you who have no money,
>   come, buy and eat!
> Come, buy wine and milk
>   without money and without price.
> Why do you spend your money for that which is not bread,
>   and your labor for that which does not satisfy?
> Hearken diligently to me, and eat what is good,
>   and delight yourself in fatness. (Isa. 55:1–2)

11. The Danger of Possessions

I love Bloomingdale's. It's the best store in the world. Beautiful, thick rugs for sale. Oriental carpets. Furniture not made of plastic. Pans that are beautiful as well as practical. Drapes almost as fine as an autumn afternoon. I'd like to furnish our whole house with things from Bloomingdale's.

"And God saw everything that he had made, and behold it was very good" (Gen. 1:31). The physical world, beauty, and Bloomingdale's are all part of God's good creation.

Yet Jesus is always warning us against possessions. In the Old Testament, possessions and wealth are often seen as blessings from God, but in the New Testament they are more often seen as some kind of problem. Did Jesus consider the physical world inferior? Was he an ascetic? Did he reverse what Moses and the Prophets taught? What is going on here?

Scripture has various strands of teaching on possessions (as well as on other topics). It would be a great mistake to try to turn those multiple strands into a single strand by forcing them to harmonize; Jesus surely understood things not given to Moses and Jeremiah.

But in any case the tension between Jesus and the Old Testament on possessions is not as great as it might seem at first. At the very least, Jesus was not an ascetic. His objection to possessions was not based on a belief in the inferiority of the material world. He was always attending feasts and dinners[1] and it's unlikely that his hosts fed him only soybeans and carrot juice.

Jesus seemed to like the physical world rather than to condemn it. Certainly he enjoyed his food and drink. The Pharisees even complained that he was "a glutton and a drunkard" (Luke 7:34; see also 5:33).

Yet without doubt Jesus considered possession dangerous. His clearest statement of this is from the Sermon on the Plain:

Blessed are you poor, for yours is the kingdom of God.
Blessed are you that hunger now, for you shall be satisfied.
But woe to you that are rich, for you have received your consolation.
Woe to you that are full now, for you shall hunger.

(Luke 6:20–21, 24–25)

Jesus' objection seems to have been not to physical things as such but to our attitude toward them. Things aren't bad, but they tend to take over our lives; our desires grow like weeds, choking out the plants of value. At least that's what the parable of the sower says, in part. The seed is choked by "the cares of the world and the delight in riches" (Matt. 13:22) or, as Luke puts it, by "the cares and riches and pleasures of life" (8:14). Riches and possessions compete with God's word to grow in our lives, and if we're not careful, they push out what counts. If we give just a little priority to money, if we set aside just a little corner of the garden for it, it soon controls the garden. Weeds grow better than flowers. That's their danger.

The story of the rich young ruler makes the same point. In that story Jesus says, "It will be hard for a rich person to enter the kingdom of heaven. Again, I tell you, it is easier for a camel to go through the eye of a needle than for a rich person to enter the kingdom of God" (Matt. 19:23–24). The rich young ruler desired to keep his things, and that pushed out God. He was unwilling to get rid of them to follow Jesus. He kept a few weeds, and they took over.

In *Perelandra* C. S. Lewis imagines an Adam and Eve living on floating islands of vegetation. There is solid ground, but they are forbidden to stay overnight on it. Sometimes the islands break up, but Adam and Eve still are not to move to land. If they did they might come to trust in the solid land and themselves. On the floating islands, they are bound to rely on God.

That is what Jesus is saying about possessions: if we have them, we trust them. Jesus wants us to have little enough that we realize that only God will be able to keep us afloat (Matt. 6:26–29).

Notice that whenever Jesus talks of possessions, he also talks of God. For to him they are the same topic—or rather the opposite topic. He not only condemns possessions; he also offers us God. But unfortunately this point is not always grasped by those who see the limits of possessions. Even Christians may rid themselves of possessions without realizing that a good deal of the point is for the empty space to be filled with God.

Whom will we trust, God or possessions? Bloomingdale's is lovely, but the things they sell don't fill the empty spaces.

How much is Jesus in conflict with the Old Testament? All the world religions are to some degree suspicious of wealth and possessions. Monks the world over take vows of poverty. So it would be surprising if Judaism didn't have some trace of this suspicion. It would be even more surprising since Jesus was himself a Jew, and his teaching was rooted firmly in that tradition.

Yet the primary thrust of the Old Testament in relation to possessions is that those who follow the way of the Lord will prosper. From Genesis to Malachi the children of Israel are taught that both personally and nationally obedience will result in boundless prosperity and disobedience in utter devastation.

Genesis makes a big point of the vast wealth of Abraham (13:1–7), Isaac (26:12–14), Jacob (30:43), and Joseph (39:2–6; 45:13). The report on Isaac is typical: "The Lord blessed him, and the man became rich and gained more and more until he became very wealthy. He had possessions of flocks and herds and a great household, so that the Philistines envied him" (26:12, 13–14). The same kinds of things (or their parallel in desolation) are said, for example, of Joshua (Josh. 1:7–8), Eli (1 Sam. 2:25), Saul (1 Sam. 13:13–14), David (2 Sam. 22:20–26), Solomon (1 Kings 3:3–14; 4:7–34), Uzziah (2 Chron. 26:1–21),

Hezekiah (2 Chron. 32:27–30), Job (Job 42:10–17), and Daniel (Dan. 2:26–30, 46–49). And psalm after psalm says that the righteous will prosper and the unrighteous wither, or else they question why the unrighteous appear to be prospering more than the righteous. (For starters, see Pss. 1–7, 9–14.)

These passages are more or less about individuals, but the promise and threat for the nation are equally clear. The classic statement is Deuteronomy 28:

> If you obey the voice of the Lord your God, being careful to do all the commandments which I command you this day, the Lord your God will set you high above all the nations of the earth. The Lord will cause your enemies who rise up against you to be defeated before you; they shall come out against you one way and flee before you seven ways. The Lord will make you abound in prosperity.
>
> But if you will not obey the voice of the Lord your God, the Lord will send you curses, confusion, and frustration, in all that you undertake to do. And the heavens over you shall be brass and the earth under you iron. The Lord will cause you to be defeated before your enemies; you shall go out one way against them and flee seven ways before them. You shall be driven mad by the sight which your eyes shall see. (Deut. 28:1, 7, 11, 15, 20, 23, 25, 34)[2]

These passages give no hint that possessions are a danger. They stand in stark contrast to "Blessed are the poor" and "Woe to the rich." The Jewish Scriptures are quite at home with Bloomingdale's, providing the customers are people who keep the commandments.

Jesus, of course, was not so comfortable with Bloomingdale's. He would probably have expected the ungodly to be at Bloomingdale's and the godly to be calling them to repentance.

However, the picture I have painted of the Old Testament, the one usually painted, is a partial picture. The Old Testament in fact gives a good many warnings against riches. As we have seen, the Old Testament repeatedly condemns coveting, and it is quite clear on the low priority possessions should take. And throughout the Old Testament, people are denounced for wanting money so badly that they take bribes or oppress the poor. So the Old Testament's rejection of wealth as a valid priority, and its awareness that greed can lead to oppression are seeds from which Jesus' distrust of possessions could grow.

Furthermore, like Jesus, the Old Testament in places acknowledges the danger of trusting possessions rather than God. My favorite statement of this is in Deuteronomy 8:

The Lord your God is bringing you into a good land, a land of brooks of waters, a land in which you will eat bread without scarcity. And you shall eat and be full, and you shall bless the Lord your God.

Take heed, lest when you have eaten and are full and have built goodly houses and live in them, and when your herds and flocks multiply, and your silver and gold is multiplied, then your heart be lifted up, and you forget the Lord your God. Beware lest you say in your heart, "My power and the might of my hand have gotten me this wealth." You shall remember the Lord your God, for it is God who gives you the power to get wealth. (vv. 7, 9, 10, 11, 12–14, 17–18)

The problem with wealth is that as soon as God lets us have a little, we think we earned it ourselves. Then we think we no longer need God. (See also Deut. 6:1–15; 31:20; 32:15–18; Prov. 30:8–9; Ps. 49:6; 52:7.)

The Chronicler tells how it happened to Uzziah, one of the great kings of Judah. He conquered many of Judah's traditional enemies and became strong. He built towers and cut out cisterns. He had large herds, and in the fertile land he had farmers and vinedressers, for he loved the soil. He built up a large, well-equipped army with newly invented engines (2 Chron. 26:6–15). "And his fame spread far, for he was marvelously helped, till he was strong. But when he was strong, he grew proud, to his own destruction. For he was false to the Lord his God" (vv. 15–16). It's like Adam and Eve on Perelandra: When our feet are on solid ground, then we promptly forget God and take charge ourselves.

Hosea says the same thing, speaking at a time when Assyria is about to conquer Israel:

I am the Lord your God,
   and besides me there is no savior.
It was I who knew you in the wilderness,
   in the land of drought;
but when they were fed to the full,
   they were filled, and their heart was lifted up;
therefore they forgot me. (13:4, 5–6)

Notice the importance of God in this statement (and the others, too). Possessions are not being denounced in themselves. The trouble with them is that they replace God as the center of our lives. The idea is not so much to get them *out* of our lives as to get God *into* the center of our lives.

What Jesus did was to develop this theme in an obvious way. He taught that since riches tend to push God out, we must beware of riches. This is a natural conclusion, but one not found in the Old Testament. Instead the Old Testament urges Israel to trust God and keep possessions in proper perspective. If people normally did that, then riches would be no problem.

But people don't. It's hard for rich people to enter the kingdom of heaven, or so Jesus said. If you have a bank account, a home, social security, life insurance, a retirement plan, who needs God?

We sometimes say that there are no atheists in foxholes. But Jesus makes an even more extreme claim: He says, in effect, that there are no Christians except in foxholes (or at least very few). Only people in trouble manage to trust God.

Jesus is too drastic for us. We prefer the Old Testament idea: You needn't get rid of your riches, only be very careful not to trust them. It's the same as with motorcycles: People who ride them tend to get hurt in accidents. But that's no reason not to ride them, only a reason to be very careful. . . .

Or so they say.

12. Sell Your Possessions

But does Jesus really teach that we should get rid of our possessions? Are they like a motorcycle—too dangerous to ride?

People heatedly disagree on this question. I suspect that part of the disagreement and most of the heat is because a yes answer would tread on the toes of almost everyone who discusses it. (It certainly would tread on mine.) That makes it hard to face the question openly and honestly.

Besides, the question is genuinely complex. Jesus has a stereoscopic view of reality, and reality (especially moral reality) is complex. As a result, Jesus' teaching often has several strands, and those strands may be in tension with one another. Furthermore, the Gospels give a stereoscopic view of Jesus. Different Gospels bring out different aspects of his teaching; they emphasize different strands.

One of the strands about possessions teaches that we should get rid of them. It is not the only strand, but it is there, and Christians need to face up to it if we are to be at all faithful to Christ.

That strand is especially strong in Luke, so let's see what that Gospel has to say.

For a start, the disciples gave all. Luke records how Peter, James, and John quit fishing, left *everything*, and followed Jesus (Luke 5:1–11). The same sort of thing is said of Levi. He was a tax collector, not a chief tax collector, but a tax collector; so he was fairly well off. But he left his job in response to Jesus' call (5:27–28).

Of course, these calls were to specific people for specific tasks. The call to the disciples was to people for whom Jesus had special plans. And obviously, we are not called to follow

Jesus physically. So the fact that the disciples left everything doesn't "prove" that we should. These calls do seem to me, however, to set the stage for a renunciation of possessions. From that point on, selling your possessions isn't a surprising call for anyone deciding to take Jesus seriously.

The stage is set further when a man tells Jesus he wants to follow him, and Jesus replies: "Foxes have holes, and birds of the air have nests; but the Son of man has nowhere to lay his head" (Luke 9:57–58). In other words, if you follow me, you'll have to give up your house, your security, maybe even your pillow; you won't know where you'll be tomorrow night.

This too is a call to a specific person and might not apply generally. However, it is the first in a series of three responses Jesus makes to people wanting to follow him, and the third is put in the form of a general principle that applies to everyone: "No one who puts hand to plow and looks back is fit for the kingdom of God" (9:62). So probably the first response also applies to everyone who wants to serve God faithfully.

In the Sermon on the Plain, Luke has a cluster of sayings that are not usually thought of as teaching us to get rid of our possessions, but if they are taken seriously, they would have that result.

If someone takes your coat do not withhold even your shirt. Give to everyone who begs from you, and if someone takes away your goods do not ask them again. (6:29, 30)

If we followed these commands literally, we would soon be free of our possessions. That is sometimes given as a reason why they can't be meant literally, but that scarcely follows. Of course, I have argued (chapter 8) that these verses are not literalistic rules but a new logic of behavior—a logic of open-handed generosity rather than of white-knuckled defense of property and rights. But this logic is no less demanding than rules. It cuts deeper and, if followed, might also rid us of our possessions.

I suggest that Luke's Beatitudes, which come right before these sayings, also point in the direction of giving away our possessions. "Blessed are the poor" and "Woe to the rich" (6:20, 24) seem to me to imply rather strongly that rich people would do well to get rid of most of their possessions.

Then there is Luke 12:13–34, the most extended passage in the New Testament on possessions. Most of it does not directly teach that we should sell all, but it says strong things about possessions that culminate (or at least end) in the command to sell our possessions.

It starts with a man asking Jesus to tell the man's brother to divide his inheritance with him. Jesus refuses on the grounds that possessions aren't important enough to bother with: "Beware of all covetousness, for a person's life does not consist in the abundance of possessions" (v. 15). For some reason, perhaps because we've heard it so often, we're liable to miss the radical nature of this response. The man may only have been asking for justice, yet Jesus calls him covetous and tells him he should suffer wrong rather than fight for his rights. He tells the man that economics is so unimportant that he should be sublimely disinterested. And anyone who felt that way would, I suspect, soon be free of possessions.

Then Jesus tells an extraordinary parable. A rich man's harvest was superabundant, and he had nowhere to store his crops. So he decided to pull down his barns and build bigger ones that would hold the whole harvest. He congratulated himself for having goods that would last him for years, and he told himself he'd take his ease; he'd eat, drink, and be merry (vv. 16–19):

But God said to him, "Fool, this night your soul is required of you; and the things you have prepared, whose will they be? So are they who lay up treasures for themselves and are not rich toward God." (vv. 20–21)

The extraordinary thing about this parable is that the man hasn't done anything "bad." He has only done what an ordinary farmer would do, what any competent businessman would do without hesitation. He hasn't stolen his neighbor's grain; he hasn't underpaid his help; he has simply had a good harvest and saved the proceeds for his own enjoyment.

Like the man squabbling over his inheritance, he has his priorities wrong. He's investing in his own ease and security ("goods laid up for many years") when he should be investing his life in God.

Jesus tells us to have a sublime contempt for our own prosperity, security, and ease. Such things just don't matter. (And if we took him seriously, how many possessions do you think we'd have?)

Jesus then goes on to talk about the ravens and the lilies. We've looked at this as it appears in the Sermon on the Mount, but notice how drastic it is. He tells the disciples not to be anxious over possessions, and we usually think we're living up to this injunction providing we aren't suffering from nervous exhaustion worrying over our possessions.

But what Jesus says is, "Do not be anxious about your life, what you shall eat, nor about your body, what you shall put on. For life is more than food, and the body more than clothing" (vv. 22–23). Do you notice anything odd about these verses? I don't know about you, but I don't worry about what I'll eat or wear, and it isn't because I'm obedient to Jesus. It's because I'm affluent enough that I *know* how I'll get my food and clothes; I'll pay for them out of my salary. I don't need to worry. I think I'm doing well if I don't worry about the needs of the affluent—such as how to save enough for a comfortable retirement or how to pay for the kids' college bills or whether I can afford an addition to the house. But Jesus is talking about bare necessities, and that's what's odd about these verses. He assumes that his disciples will be living at an economic level where even food and clothes are a problem—and they aren't supposed to worry about it.

In other words, they'll have next to no possessions.

But the drastic implications don't stop there. Jesus points the disciples to the ravens and lilies. The ravens "neither sow nor reap," and (unlike the rich fool) "they have neither storehouse nor barn" (v. 24). The lilies "neither toil nor spin" (v. 27). They, rather than the rich fool, are to be our models. We don't need storehouses and savings accounts and secure jobs. Like the ravens and lilies, we will be taken care of. And ravens and lilies don't have any possessions.

Then, lest we not understand his imagery, Jesus says it explicitly: "Do not seek what you are to eat or what you are to drink" (v. 29). Even basic necessities are beneath our concern. (Where do you suppose that leaves closetsful of possessions?) "Instead seek God's kingdom and these things will be yours as well" (v.31). Everything but God's kingdom is irrelevant, is of sublime disinterest. God will provide what the passage has been discussing, but that is practically nothing. It is not the yachts and Cadillacs we sometimes imagine—it is merely food, clothing, drink. No mention of closetsful of possessions. Jesus here promises only the bare necessities.

Then comes the conclusion:

> Fear not, little flock, for it is the Father's good pleasure to give you the kingdom. Sell your possessions and give alms. (vv. 32–33)

After all that Jesus has said in Luke 12, this seems like the natural conclusion.

It was inevitable.

The story of the rich young ruler is perhaps the best-known place where Jesus tells someone to sell their possessions (Luke 18:18–30). You know the story. A ruler came to Jesus asking how to inherit eternal life, and Jesus told him to obey the commandments. When the ruler said he already did, Jesus told him, "Sell all that you have and distribute to the poor" (v. 22).

The most amazing thing about this story is not the story itself but how we interpret it. We stumble over ourselves explaining that it doesn't apply to everyone; it's only for greedy people like the rich young ruler. This command, we say, was given only to the rich young ruler, not to anyone else in the Gospels.

This sudden enthusiasm for situational ethics always intrigues me, but it's false that Jesus didn't tell anyone else to sell their possessions. We've just seen that this is what Jesus taught in Luke 12. To all intents and purposes, it is what Jesus meant when he said the Son of man had nowhere to lay his head, and it is also the way the disciples understood the call to follow Jesus (as their discussion about the rich young ruler shows, vv. 28–30). And Luke 14:33 says the same thing, as we shall see.

In any case, the story goes on to make the point in a general way. "How hard it is for those who have riches to enter the kingdom of God" (v. 24). It may be that only the greedy rich need to sell their possessions, but if so, Jesus must think it's almost inevitable for rich people to be greedy: They generally have a hard time entering the kingdom.

But then Jesus says something odd, given that he's just told a man to sell his possessions. He tells the disciples that anyone who has left house or family for the sake of the kingdom will receive even more houses and family. Is this a promise that if the ruler sold his possessions he'd get even more possessions? Is Jesus agreeing with those parts of the Old Testament that promise boundless economic success?

I think not. In the first place, many missionaries and some other Christians leave houses and family and yet live their lives in modest circumstances; they don't necessarily own a summer house as well as a regular one. Jesus seems rather to have radically reinterpreted the world and the Old Testament. For him the family is no longer blood relatives: "My mother and my brothers are those who hear the word of God" (8:21). So to have a bigger family than the one you've left is to have a multitude of close ties to other followers of Jesus. And to have more houses is not to possess more real estate; it is to have access to an array of homes of other Christians. In the curious way Jesus has of transforming and fulfilling the Old Testament, Jesus promises enriched lives rather than riches.

But this promise is for those who sell their possessions.

Then in another passage, one found only in Luke, Jesus says, "Whoever you are, if you do not renounce all that you possess, you cannot be my disciple" (14:33). (Most translations say "all that you have" but lest we try to weasel out of its meaning, the Greek says "possess.")

Before talking about renouncing possessions, Jesus says you don't build a tower without first counting the cost to be sure you can afford to finish it. Then Jesus says "*Therefore,* whoever you are, if you don't renounce all your possessions, you cannot be my disciple." In other words, one of the conditions of being his disciple is to get rid of your possessions, and unless you're going to do it, don't bother to start following him. Don't start building this tower unless you intend to finish it by selling all.

Most of the sayings about possessions are said to the inner circle of disciples or to someone especially rich, but this passage is directed to a "great multitude" (v. 25). This is a universal call. It can't possibly be understood to be intended only for the especially greedy, the especially holy, or for those especially initiated into a particular calling. It applies to us all.

Remember the poor widow (21:1–4)? She only gave two copper coins. Meanwhile rich people were putting in large gifts out of their abundance. But Jesus didn't commend them—they still had an abundance left over. He commended the poor widow, for she "put in all the living that she had" (v. 4). She gave all.

Without doubt, one strand of Jesus' teaching is that we should sell all. And in Luke it is a major strand.[1]

Luke 5, 6, 9, 12, 14, 18, 21.

Enough said.

13. The Zacchaeus Connection

Selling everything is not the only strand in Jesus' teaching about possessions. Another strand emphasizes using possessions properly—keeping some and being generous with the rest. I'll call that the Zacchaeus connection.

Zacchaeus—the wee little man of Sunday school fame. He was a chief tax collector: He was the boss of tax collectors, like Levi. So he was wealthy, very wealthy. He was also a cheat and a quizzling (he worked for the hated Romans). But to the horror of the Jews, Jesus sought Zacchaeus out and went home with him. Then out of the clear blue, Zacchaeus announced that he was giving half his wealth to the poor and repaying the people he had cheated four times over.

Jesus might have said that that wasn't good enough; he might have insisted that Zacchaeus sell all. But he didn't. He said, "Today salvation has come to this house" (Luke 19:9).

And Zacchaeus is not the only disciple who didn't sell all his possessions. Joseph of Arimathea, the man who provided Jesus' tomb, is perhaps the most obvious example (Luke 23:50, 53), and Nicodemus, who was probably also wealthy (John 19:39–42), is another. Meanwhile Martha, one of Jesus' best-known followers, held on to her house (Luke 10:38). And, whatever Luke may say, in John's Gospel Peter still has a boat after he left all (John 21:3).

But frankly, these examples are not all that compelling. Joseph and Nicodemus were both secret disciples (John 19:38; 7:45–52)—hardly models for us to follow. (In fact, one wonders if it was their wealth and status that kept them from being all-out followers of Jesus.) And just after Luke mentions Martha's house, he reports that Jesus rebuked her for being "anxious" (10:41)—the very attitude toward possessions that Jesus warns against (Luke 12:21–22). Also, Peter's boat was quite possibly a family boat that he had no right to sell. In any case, mightn't Peter have been better off without access to the boat? Then, in times of discouragement, he wouldn't have had a way to leave his calling and return to fishing.

If anything, these examples seem to me to be part of the strand teaching us to sell all, not part of the Zacchaeus connection. They underline how desirable it is not to have possessions.

But the Zacchaeus connection *is* illustrated by a group of wealthy women who traveled with Jesus. Luke tells us of Joanna, the wife of "Herod's steward, and Susanna and many others, who provided for [Jesus and the disciples] out of their means" (8:1–3). So here is a group of women of means who share generously, but who have not sold their possessions. Of course, the wealth may well have been controlled by their husbands and not been theirs to sell . . . but then again that may not have been the case.

In any case the Zacchaeus story is fairly clear. However, even that story isn't primarily about possessions. Its point is that the socially and morally disreputable can enter the kingdom—whatever the Pharisees may think (Luke 19:7, 10). And I am tempted to argue that we have here only the start of Zacchaeus' journey, a dramatic start at that—one that might well lead to his selling all. But the fact is, he didn't sell all to start with—which makes the point that not all possessions always have to be sold.

And the stories of Nicodemus, of Joseph of Arimathea, and of Martha also make that point: You can follow Jesus, at least after a fashion, and still have possessions. They were genuine followers, if not ideal ones. And Zacchaeus, Joanna, and Susanna were almost ideal.

Several other passages are also said to support the Zacchaeus connection implicitly. Jesus advocates giving alms, and, the argument runs, to give alms you have to have something to give. However, in his two clear commendations of almsgiving, the alms are to come from selling possessions (Luke 12:33, 18:22). So the claim seems to backfire.

People also say that having possessions is implied in the cluster of sayings like "Give to everyone who begs from you" (Luke 6:30). But this reasoning truly seems to be grasping at straws. As I've argued, giving to all beggars would be an effective way of getting rid of your possessions.

According to some, the parable of the dishonest steward (Luke 16:1–13) is an endorsement of possessions. This is probably Jesus' most obscure parable, and I won't discuss it in detail here. Suffice it to say that, according to most scholars, it probably means that we should act decisively and use our money well by being generous, which is different from telling us to sell all. However, Jesus is counseling drastic action; he seems to be saying that the point of money is not our own gratification but using it for God by helping others, for example. If we took that attitude, wouldn't we soon be without possessions? And Luke's comments on the parable end with, "You cannot serve God and mammon" (v. 13). This comment seems to be calling for a decisive choice against possessions—not endorsing keeping them.

Jesus' enjoyment of feasts, with their food and drink, is a more likely endorsement of possessions. But I suspect it's significant that it's always someone else's feast he enjoys; other's feasts don't oblige him to have the hassle of possessions. On the other hand, he doesn't try to stop the feasts—he doesn't tell people they should be too poor to have feasts. In Luke 14:12–14 Jesus tells one of his hosts to invite poor people to his feasts, which introduces a drastic note typical of Jesus' extreme teaching, but this suggestion still presumes keeping possessions.

Also in Luke, just before his arrest, Jesus gives what seems to be strong support for the Zacchaeus connection. Previously he had sent out the twelve (9:1–6) and the seventy (10:1–12); they were to travel around, teaching and healing, without taking along money or even extra clothes. This injunction clearly suggests that disciples should have no possessions. But then Jesus seems to countermand these orders:

"When I sent you out with no purse or bag or sandals, did you lack anything?" They said, "Nothing." He said to them, "But now let him who has a purse take it, and likewise a bag. And let him who has no sword sell his mantle and buy one. For I tell you that this scripture must be fulfilled in me, 'And he was reckoned with transgressors'; for what is written about me has its fulfilment." And they said, "Look, Lord, here are two swords." And he said to them, "It is enough." (Luke 22:35–38)

What can this passage mean? Does Jesus here reverse all he has taught about getting rid of possessions? Did those teachings only apply up to his arrest? There is a near consensus among commentators that it means no such thing. Rather Jesus is telling his disciples that up till now they have been well received, but now that is all about to change. From now on they'll have to fight for what they believe. Jesus doesn't mean that they should literally start fighting with swords or literally start saving money, but his disciples think this is what he means. So they tell him they've already got two swords, and Jesus says that that is enough.

This statement would be ridiculous if he meant it literally. Two swords would be irrelevant or dangerous against the soldiers of the Sanhedrin. Besides, when Peter does try to use his literal sword a little later, Jesus rebukes him. Some commentators go so far as to say that when Jesus said, "It is enough," what he meant was that he'd had enough of the disciples' stupidity.

In the rest of the New Testament, the Zacchaeus connection is a stronger strand. The first three Gospels, and possibly the beginning of Acts, are the only places in the New Testament (indeed in the whole Bible) that sometimes teach selling all. The rest of the New Testament takes a dim view of possessions, but not to the extent of suggesting getting rid of them. Thus Paul says:

I have learned in whatever state I am, to be content. I know how to be abased, and I know how to abound; in any and all circumstances I have learned the secret of facing plenty and hunger, abundance and want. (Phil. 4:11–12)

And when Paul advises Timothy what to tell the wealthy, he doesn't advise telling them to sell all:

As for the rich in this world, charge them not to be haughty, nor to set their hopes on uncertain riches but on God who richly furnishes us with everything to enjoy. They are to do good, to be rich in good deeds, liberal and generous, thus laying up for themselves a good foundation for the future, so that they may take hold of the life which is life indeed. (1 Tim. 6:17–19)

A clearer statement of the Zacchaeus connection could hardly be made.

So the Zacchaeus connection may be a weak strand in the teaching of Jesus as portrayed in the first three Gospels, but it is a stronger strand in Paul.

But what exactly is the Zacchaeus connection? Sometimes people recognize that it doesn't demand disposing of all possessions, and they use that to justify keeping *everything*. They read the Zacchaeus story, and they don't say, "He gave away half his goods, and then some; I'll do the same." Instead they say, "He kept nearly half his goods, so why should I give anything away?"

Which is perverse.

That reasoning reminds me of the man who told me that since Jesus had a valuable, seamless robe, possessions must not be a problem. Now in the first place, popular belief notwithstanding, seamless robes were not especially valuable; common people wore them. But even if they were valuable, the argument is bizarre. It would mean that at the end of his life all Jesus owned was one good set of clothes—and that's extremely little.

To conclude from this point that it's all right to own twelve outfits, two cars, a summer home, and a swimming pool is a little odd. A more reasonable conclusion would be that we should get rid of most everything we own.

And that I think is the Zacchaeus connection.

Paul certainly seems to suggest that we should get rid of most all our possessions. In the passage previously quoted from 1 Timothy, Paul doesn't tell the rich to sell all, but he's clearly worried about the rich. Just as he implies that they may keep their wealth, he also implies that they are liable to be haughty, liable to trust their riches instead of God, liable not to be really living. For Paul, money is distracting, dangerous tinsel.

Paul may not have advocated selling all, but he might as well have. For Paul, money is beneath contempt. He wouldn't walk across the street to get a million dollars for himself.

When he says in Philippians that he has "learned the secret of facing plenty and hunger," he may in part be endorsing wealth but primarily he is endorsing his own poverty. They have sent him a gift and he's rejoicing in it, but he tells them not to worry about his being hungry before he got their gift: He has learned to cope with hunger and want. He doesn't even seek their gift except that by giving they benefit themselves (Phil. 4:10–19). After all, he counts "everything as loss"; in fact, he has already lost "all things and counts them as garbage in order [to] gain Christ" (Phil. 3:8). In this verse Paul is referring primarily to things like circumcision, but presumably he includes money. Money is garbage.

Jesus is all that's worth crossing the street for. That is the core of the Zacchaeus principle—not holding on to as much as you can.

Go, sell most all your possessions.

What are we to make of all this? Jesus is so confusing. He tells the rich young ruler to sell all, but he's delighted when Zacchaeus gets rid of half. How much are we allowed to keep anyway? If we're generous, can we keep quite a lot? How generous do we have to be? What's the rule here?

Such questions make nonsense of Jesus' teaching. He was not trying to give us an ethical system from which we could deduce details of how to act. As I argued in Part II, Jesus wasn't giving us rules to memorize.

He was trying to *do* something to us. His teaching was meant to alter our perception of reality. He wanted us to have a change of heart, a reversal of values. And many of the questions I have been asking grow out of an old understanding of reality that needs to be turned on its head. I have been asking, Do we have to sell all, or will selling half do? But that question is all wrong.

For one thing Jesus isn't inclined to give us the packaged, predigested answers we want. He wants us to struggle with questions ourselves. Genuine insights have to be worked through, not memorized from a catechism.

Things don't look the same out of the left eye as they do out of the right eye. The difference of perspective between the two eyes is part of what adds depth to perception. Jesus hoped to give us such a stereoscopic view of reality by teaching different perspectives; he leaves tensions and differences. A view of reality without paradox is not a view of reality at all.

Besides, Jesus and the rest of the New Testament are trying to get through our heads the irrelevance and unimportance of wealth. We may imagine Jesus is setting up hurdles to see how high we can jump, but in fact he's trying to free us. He's telling us that possessions are meaningless tinsel. The doorway to life, as paradoxical as it may seem to us, is turning our backs on money and ourselves.

The real question is not how much tinsel can we keep, but rather how much can we get rid of.

4. MONEY AND BEYOND

14. Sharing

Remember the little girl I saw in the Philippines? The one getting paper cups out of the trash? If I sell my possessions, what good will that do her? What good will it do the forty thousand kids who will die today because they are poor?

Now I believe we should free ourselves of possessions for our own sakes whether it helps the poor or not. The effect on the poor and oppressed is therefore not the only question, but it is one question—an important one. And one answer is obvious: If we sell our possessions and spend less on ourselves, we will have more to give to others. This theme occurs frequently in the Bible, so frequently that those Christians suspicious of giving to the poor have no claim to being biblical Christians.

In Deuteronomy, the second code of the law, the Israelites were told to give a tithe of their crops. Today, if we think of tithes at all, we think of giving to the church, but in Israel tithes were given to the Levites (the church, so to speak) *and* the poor (Deut. 14:22–29; 26:12–13). At festival times, the Israelites were to involve not just their families in their feasts and celebrations but also the poor. And when they harvested, they were to leave some of the crop behind for the poor (23:19–22).

They were also to lend generously to the poor:

If there are among you poor people in the land which the Lord your God gives you, you shall not harden your heart or shut your hand, but you shall lend them sufficient for their need, whatever it may be. You shall give to them freely, and your heart shall not be grudging. You shall open wide your hand to your brothers and sisters, to the poor and to the needy in the land. (Deut. 15:7, 8, 10, 11)

The spirit was to be one of openhanded sharing, not of white-knuckled duty.[1]

But the most passionate words are perhaps in Isaiah:

> Is not this the fast that I choose:
>   to share your bread with the hungry,
>   and to bring the homeless poor into your house? (58:6, 7)

Instead of buying myself lunch, I should have given my change to that Filipino girl.

In the New Testament the emphasis on sharing with the poor is both more common and more pungent than in the Old Testament. The rich young ruler was told to sell his possessions and give to the poor, and Zacchaeus gave half his goods to the poor. Once Jesus told the crowd to sell their possessions and give alms (Luke 12:33). In Matthew, Jesus says to give to those who beg (5:42), and in Luke the statement is even stronger—"Give to *everyone* who begs from you" (6:30). Apparently Jesus and the disciples practiced what they preached, for they kept a common purse from which they gave to the poor (Mark 14:3–9; Matt. 26:6–13; John 12:1–8, 13:29).

But the most moving statement on giving to the poor is Jesus' account of the judgment:

Then the King will say to those at his right hand, "Come, O blessed of my Father, inherit the kingdom prepared for you from the foundation of the world; for I was hungry and you gave me food, I was thirsty and you gave me drink, I was a stranger and you welcomed me, I was naked and you clothed me. I was sick and you visited me, I was in prison and you came to me." Then the righteous will answer him, "Lord, when did we see you hungry and feed you, or thirsty and give you drink? And when did we see you a stranger and welcome you, or naked and clothe you? And when did we see you sick or in prison and visit you?" And the King will answer them, "Truly, I say to you, as you did it to one of the least of these my brothers and sisters, you did it to me." Then he will say to those at his left hand, "Depart from me, you cursed, into the eternal fire prepared for the devil and his angels; for I was hungry and you gave me no food, I was thirsty, and you gave me no drink. . . ." (Matt. 25:34–42)

Jesus cared deeply about sharing with the poor. In fact, he said that those who don't share will go to hell.[2]

Acts and the Epistles also often talk about sharing with the poor, sometimes in strong language. If I had to pick one verse that says it all, I'd pick 1 John 3:17: "If you have the world's goods and see your brothers and sisters in need, yet close your heart against them, how does God's love abide in you?"
What else is there to say?

The New Testament proposes sharing as a way of life. But notice carefully that it offers no program that must be followed in detail. That doesn't mean, however, that we get off lightly. The New Testament makes some drastic suggestions: holding property in common, having a common purse, sharing till we all have equal resources, selling all, giving half. Christians need not follow any of these programs legalistically; in fact, we shouldn't. We shouldn't calculate the average income of Christians in the United States and in Bangladesh and then give till we all have exactly the same number of dollars. That would be contrary to the spirit of generosity reflected throughout the Bible. (So perhaps we should do more.)
But at the least, the New Testament's sharing programs are models of the sorts of responses we should make, and our responses should be equally drastic. The New Testament doesn't offer programs to be copied, but it does offer a mindset to work toward: We are to be totally economically available to others in the Christian community; we are to accept unlimited economic liability for them.[3]
So what will it be? A common purse, having everything in common, giving half of what you own to the poor, selling all? Or do you have some equally drastic and compassionate plan of your own? Anything less is selling the Bible short.

So the solution to poverty, and most of the world's other problems, is sharing money? It seems obvious. If people are poor, they need money. And if you're opposed to the bomb, raise money to campaign against it.

Yet that kind of solution has an oddly materialistic ring to it. It would mean Christians should be going out and getting higher paying jobs so we'd have more to share.

So Jesus should have said to the rich young ruler, "Listen, you have a great opportunity. Invest your money well and give the profits to me and the poor. You could be of tremendous use in my cause. We've been looking for someone to bankroll us. Maybe you could even become president of the Chase-Jerusalem Bank. Then you'd really have clout for me and the poor."

But can anyone really imagine Jesus saying that? Some people claim that the only reason Jesus didn't say that to the rich young ruler was that the rich young ruler was too attached to his possessions. However, the fact is that Jesus never said any such thing to *anyone*. That just isn't what he was doing. Nowhere in Scripture is anyone ever told to get rich, either to help the poor or for any other reason.

Jesus does tell the parable of the talents, and that parable is sometimes taken to mean we should invest our money to get a big return. That *is* what it says literally. The master gives money to his servants, and on his return he wants to know whether they have increased it (Matt. 25:14–30; see also Luke 19:11–27). But that parable is no more about money than the preceding one (the ten virgins) is about what virgins should do at weddings. They are both parables.

The parable of the talents teaches that we should develop the gifts God has given us. Of course, if we're gifted at making money, then perhaps we should develop that gift and give what we earn to the poor. That's a reasonable argument.

But clearly we aren't to develop all the gifts we have. Actors shouldn't develop their skills to become con artists, and women shouldn't rent out their bodies in order to give the proceeds to the poor. Some talents are wrong or dangerous and shouldn't be developed.

To decide whether we should develop the gift of earning money, we have to ask whether the New Testament treats earning money as the sort of gift we should develop or as dangerous and irrelevant.

As I've already said, earning money is one gift the New Testament never tells us to develop. In fact, Jesus never says anything good about money, nor does he qualify his censures by adding "except for those who plan to give to the poor." What he tells us is that it's hard for rich people to enter the kingdom (Matt. 19:23). So it's scarcely surprising that Jesus doesn't urge people to get rich in order to give it away.

Paul is a little more complicated. He does say, "Let the thief no longer steal, but rather let him labor, doing honest work with his hands, so that he may be able to give to those in need" (Eph. 4:28). Here a man is to earn money in order to share with the poor. But I don't think Paul is primarily dealing with poverty relief here. It's a case of some Christian either sponging off the Christian community or else actually stealing for a living. Paul is telling him to pull his own weight, in fact to do more than pull his own weight because it is better to give than to receive. And in any case, Paul is not urging him to get rich, only to earn a living.

So the New Testament never encourages us to get rich— even in order to use our money well.

In fact, Jesus seems to have been at least as concerned *that* we dispose of our possessions as he was that we dispose of them by giving them to the poor. Clarence Jordan tells of a wealthy woman coming to him to ask what to do with her money. He claims to have told her he thought she should throw it in the river, and being who he was he probably did. I don't think Jesus ever went that far, but Jordan's suggestion is closer to his spirit than the idea of investing wisely so we'll have more to give.

Thus Jesus commends the widow though she gave only two pennies, and he ignores the rich people who gave much. The effect of what the widow gave would be slight—much less than the effect of what the rich gave—but the effect is not what matters to Jesus. What matters is that she gave all (Luke 21: 1–4). She got rid of what she had.

Jesus has three extended discussions of money. One is in the Sermon on the Mount (Matt. 6:19–34), and in the verses on money he never even mentions the poor. The Sermon's point is that we are not to treasure, serve, or pursue money, and surely Jesus wouldn't want us to treasure, serve, or pursue money even if we planned to give it to the poor.

Luke 12 has a longer discussion of money, and it does mention the poor. It says, "Sell your possessions and give alms" (v. 33), but out of twenty-two verses that's only a fraction of one verse devoted to the poor. Once again the focus is not on the poor but on not hoarding possessions, on not thinking they're central, on not worrying about them.

The third major discussion of riches is connected with the rich young ruler. In it the poor are mentioned. Jesus tells the rich young ruler to sell his possessions and give to the poor. But the discussion afterwards with the disciples makes it clear that the key is renouncing possessions, not giving them to the poor. He tells the disciples that those who have left homes and families will receive great reward, and he doesn't specify that they give anything to the poor (Matt. 19:27–30; Mark 10:28–31; Luke 18:28–30).

So as important as sharing with the poor is, it is not the only, or even the main reason to rid ourselves of possessions.[4]

In our materialistic society, it is easy to suppose that money will solve any problem. If we want to fight the bomb, we raise money. If we want to strengthen the family, we raise money. And naturally, if we want to alleviate poverty, we raise money. We throw money at every problem and wonder why most of them keep growing. We imagine that it is because we haven't thrown enough money.

Belief in the importance of money runs so deep in our culture that even the church accepts it. Even those who criticize the materialism of our culture and stress the importance of sharing with the poor usually think money is the key to the problem of poverty. Ironically, most Christian discussions on poverty and simple living give a materialistic analysis: Sharing money will solve the problem.

But if we are to make any progress against the horrors of our world, we're going to have to give a deeper ethical and spiritual analysis than that.

15. Money Is Not Enough

Money is not enough.

Money is crucial, but often it can't deal with the real problem. After an earthquake, people do need money (and not much else) to rebuild their houses. However, not many problems are that simple. When war makes people refugees, they need money for food and shelter, but more than that they need peace. And peace can't be bought. When people are being tortured, they may need financial help for their families, but that is not their main problem; mainly they need a government that will not tolerate torture. And money has only a limited role in producing such governments.

Most people picture social problems being caused by natural disasters—like earthquakes or droughts. And the solution is quite simple: money. Money can't prevent earthquakes, of course, nor can it make rain, but a judicious use of money will tide people over and will eventually deal with their economic problems.

Alongside this picture of natural disasters as the cause of the typical social problem goes another picture—that of America as the breadbasket of the world, generously providing relief to the needy. Any hungry person can count on relief from America.

But let me offer a contrasting picture. Consider José, one of the forty thousand kids who will die today because they are poor. José lives in Mindanao, the most southern island of the Philippines. His father was a sharecropper until President Marcos seized power. Marcos decreed that all large estates would be turned over to the little people who were actually farming them. However, he made an exception: Estates growing food for export would not be turned over. So naturally all the large estates started growing food they could export—things like sugar and bananas.

So what looked like a law to help poor people turned out to be a law to increase foreign exchange. It actually decreased the amount of food available for poor people to eat. The Philippines, like almost all countries, grows enough to feed its people, but it exports it to (among other places) the breadbasket of the world. As a result, José is dying.

You see, the estate where José's father used to sharecrop now grows bananas. And bananas do not require the intensive labor of sharecroppers; so the owner threw out the sharecroppers and bulldozed their homes. José's family has always been poor, but previously they had grown enough to feed themselves (after a fashion) whereas now they have no land for growing food. José's father is now a day laborer on the estate where he used to live, but he gets only seasonal work and often can't feed his family. Where he used to grow food for his family, the landowner now grows bananas for prosperous people in Japan and America. For people like you and me.

Now exporting is not necessarily wrong. But somehow in a standard economy the benefits never seem to trickle down to poor people like José. Without land they must become laborers, and there is a surplus of laborers; so wages stay low. The foreign exchange the bananas earned seems to have been spent mostly by the prosperous on luxury consumer goods—televisions and cars. And by the government on arms—arms bought in America. To fight guerrillas who opposed Marcos.

The United States didn't install Marcos, but it did support him almost to the end. At the World Bank and the International Monetary Fund, the United States voted for loans to the Philippines. Marcos was given U.S. foreign aid to keep the economy afloat. And we rented military bases from him.

If Christians in America sent money to José, what would it do? What if an American family "adopted" a kid like José and sent his family money through some agency? What would it accomplish?

Well, if it were properly administered, it would do some good. It would keep José alive, improve his health, and perhaps help him with schooling. But it would not provide work or land for his father. It would not increase land growing food for local use. So money will help José some, but it will not touch the root problems.

Money is not enough.

The world's problems are caused by all sorts of things. One cause is natural disasters, but that isn't the only cause. Another cause is oppression of the poor by governments, another is laziness, and another is rich countries importing food that poor countries need themselves.

This is not the place to have an extended discussion of whether the world's problems are caused by bad planning or oppression, laziness or injustice, ignorance or violence. But it is the place to ask what kind of picture of the world's problems pervades the Bible.

In the Bible problems arise when people don't worship God and obey God's law. Problems are seen as fundamentally spiritual and moral. A nation prospers and is at peace as long as it serves God. The solution to problems is never, ever irrigation to fight drought, and it is never, ever more arms to resist enemies. The solution is to return to God.

Our culture is partial to technological fixes—a new strain of wheat that will grow even during drought, a bomb that will terrify the enemy into submission, a pill that will reduce the number of children born. And such fixes are more or less available to people prepared to spend enough. But the Bible is unimpressed by such solutions, and history suggests we all should be equally unimpressed. Real solutions cannot be bought. So giving money is not the only response the Bible proposes to poverty. It also proposes fighting for justice and defending the poor from their oppressors. That is because the Bible often pictures the plight of the poor as caused by the strong taking advantage of the weak and perverting the justice due them. That picture of poverty pervades the Old Testament and fits perfectly with the story of José. What picture we have of the cause of poverty will largely decide what we think the solution will be.

That is not to say that the Old Testament ignores other causes of poverty. Drought gets mentioned (see, for example, Gen. 41:46–57), and laziness gets considerable attention, at least in Proverbs (see, for example, 6:6–11; 10:4–5; 24:30–34; and 26:13–16). But laziness and drought are not blamed with anything like the same regularity as oppression and injustice.

The Law attacks the root cause of poverty. It not only tells the Israelites to share; it also warns them not to oppress the weak. Its understanding of poverty is that it is caused by the strong treading on the weak: "You shall not wrong strangers or oppress them, for you were strangers in the land of Egypt. You shall not afflict any widow or orphan" (Exod. 22:21–22). The Law's prohibition against moving landmarks (Deut. 19:14) and using varying weights and measures (Deut. 25:13–16; Lev. 19:35–36) assumes that the comfortable will cheat the weak.

The Law demands justice for the defenseless more often than it asks for donations.[1]

The poetic books also picture oppression as a major cause of poverty. In Job how you treat the poor and defenseless is seen as crucial. And it's not just a question of whether you share with the poor but of whether you fly to their defense (29:12, 16) or crush (20:19) and strip (22:6) them. Poverty is not seen as the result of misfortune but of evil people prowling like wild animals in search of prey. So the godly person's reaction is to fight:

I was a father to the poor,
    and I searched out the cause of those I did not know.
I broke the fangs of the unrighteous
    and made them drop their prey from their teeth. (Job 29:16–17)[2]

What José needed most was someone to break Marcos' fangs. Without that, sharing is of limited value.

The Psalter has the same picture of poverty. The Psalms

lament that the powerful and the wicked pursue the godly and the poor. The righteous person's task is to leap to the defense of the needy, and the Psalms beseech God to do the same. The poor need advocates and protectors as well as money:

In arrogance the wicked hotly pursue the poor. . . .
    They lurk in secret like lions in their hiding places . . .
they lurk that they may seize the poor. . . .
The hapless commit themselves to you;
    you have been the helper of the fatherless.
Break the arm of the wicked. (Ps. 10:2, 9, 14, 15)

Psalm 72 understands the poor to be oppressed and in need of defenders:

May the king judge your people with righteousness
    and your poor with justice!
May he defend the cause of the poor of the people,
    give deliverance to the needy,
    and crush the oppressor!

For he delivers the needy when they call,
    the poor and those who have no helper.
From the oppression and violence he redeems their lives;
    and precious is their blood in his sight (72:2, 4, 12, 14).

Psalms 10 and 72 are undoubtedly two of the more colorful portrayals of this picture of poverty and of the right response to it. However, dozens of other Psalms say or imply the same sort of thing.[3]

Proverbs is perhaps best remembered for its picture of poverty caused by laziness ("Go to the ant, you sluggard"), but that is not the only picture in Proverbs. Proverbs also emphasizes the role of injustice and defending the oppressed. In fact, it devotes about the same number of verses to injustice as to laziness. And the verses about not oppressing the poor (and about the need to defend them) are unusually colorful:

The fallow ground of the poor yields much food,
    but it is swept away through injustice (13:23).

Do not rob the poor because they are poor
   or crush the afflicted at the gate;
for the Lord will plead their cause
   and despoil of life those who despoil them. (22:22–23)

Rescue those who are being taken away to death;
   hold back those whose who are stumbling to the slaughter.
(24:11)

There are those whose teeth are swords,
   whose teeth are knives,
to devour the poor from off the earth,
   the needy from among the living. (30:14)

So if we suppose that most poverty is caused by misfortune, laziness, or bad planning, then our views have not been fully informed even by Proverbs,[4] let alone by the rest of the Old Testament.

And don't forget the prophets.

They are famous for their denunciations of the rich. They do not primarily call for sharing or charity toward the poor; rather they call for an end to idolatry and injustice. They, or at least the ones dealing with such things, understand poverty as the result of the rich and powerful oppressing the poor and defenseless.

This point is probably most clearly illustrated in Amos, the first prophet to leave a written message. Amos attacks the rich women, "the cows of Bashan, who oppress the poor, who crush the needy" (4:1). And in a later chapter he says:

Hear this, you who trample upon the needy
   and bring the poor to an end
saying, "When will the new moon be over,
   that we may sell grain?
And the sabbath,
   that we may offer wheat for sale,
that we may make the ephah small and the shekel great,
   and deal deceitfully with false balances,

> that we may buy the poor for silver
> and the needy for a pair of sandals,
> and sell the refuse of the wheat?" (8:4–6)[5]

Isaiah, prophesying not long after Amos, carries on the tradition. Poverty is not due to natural disasters or laziness; it is due to oppression. The proper response is not so much sharing money as to "seek justice, correct oppression; defend the fatherless, plead for the widows" (Isa. 1:17). To Isaiah it is clear that given a chance, the strong will take advantage of the weak, and so we must defend their cause:

> The Lord enters into judgment
> with the elders and princes of his people:
> "It is you who have devoured the vineyard,
> the spoil of the poor is in your houses.
> What do you mean by crushing my people,
> by grinding the face of the poor?" (Isa. 3:14–15)[6]

The New Testament does not give quite as clear a picture of what causes poverty. Luke repeatedly denounces the rich, and that may well be partly because he thinks they got their wealth unjustly (though he never says so). In fact, given the Old Testament background, that is the most plausible reading.

And Jesus' denunciation of the scribes and Pharisees has the ring of the prophets. He says that inside the Pharisees "are full of extortion and rapacity" (Matt. 23:25; Luke 11:39), and the scribes "devour widow's houses" (Mark 12:40; Luke 20:47). Jesus' cleansing the temple also suggests oppression by officials: "It is written, 'My house shall be called a house of prayer,' but you have made it a den of robbers" (Matt. 21:13; Mark 11:17; Luke 19:46; John 2:16).

The book of Revelation is hard to understand, but this point is clear: government can be cruel and oppressive (see especially Rev. 13). In that respect Revelation is like the Old Testament prophets.

James is the one New Testament book that has a developed

sense of the rich as oppressors who hound the poor. "Is it not the rich who oppress you, is it not they who drag you into court?" asks James 2:6. And in a passage worthy of Amos, James says:

Come now, you rich, weep and howl for the miseries that are coming upon you. Behold the wages of the laborers who mowed your fields, which you kept back by fraud, cry out; and the cries of the harvesters have reached the ears of the Lord of hosts. You have lived on the earth in luxury and pleasure; you have fattened your hearts in a day of slaughter. You have condemned, you have killed the righteous; they do not resist you. (5:1, 4–6)

However, the view of the cause of poverty that pervades the Old Testament does not pervade the New Testament. As I've argued, traces of it are found in the Gospels and Revelation, and it is quite fully stated in James. But in the New Testament this view is not so common and clear. It's not that contrary views predominate; they don't. The little that is in the New Testament supports the Old. But the New Testament addresses the question only in passing.

It seems to me that we can therefore conclude that in the Bible injustice and oppression are the major causes of poverty. From a biblical point of view, José is probably poor because of oppression.

The point is that money is not enough. Giving money will not solve the world's problems. More is needed. José does need money for food and clean water and inoculations. But he also needs advocates. He needs defenders who will break the fangs of those who lie in wait for him. He needs more than wonder seeds that will grow more food, more than a techno-logical fix.

What is needed is moral and spiritual regeneration that will address problems like greed, violence, hardheartedness, cru-elty, and injustice. In addition to fund-raisers who will give him food, José needs prophets like Elijah and Amos who will make known the need to repent. In the final analysis the problem of poverty, like most social problems, is moral and spiritual much more than it is economic or technological. So José needs people who will address poverty and violence and racism in clear spiritual and moral terms.

16. Prophetic Evangelism

Learning to spend less will help free us to confront injustice. If we intend to call on the powerful to repent, we cannot expect to receive a normal income.

People who think they must earn twenty thousand dollars a year in order to make payments on their homes, cars, and living room furniture are not free to follow Jesus; they are obliged to follow money. Ministers, teachers, and politicians who speak too clearly about justice endanger their jobs; executives who object to exploitation by their company shouldn't expect promotion; laborers who work to organize their shop should expect retaliation. And anyone who wants to work full time for justice will take a pay cut.

Ed Asner is a good example. When he took a clear stand against American involvement in El Salvador, his television program, "Lou Grant," was abruptly canceled despite its popularity. Now I suspect Asner's case is unusual. Calling for justice and repentance is tolerated more than people think. But at times the ax *does* fall. Fear of this happening keeps people quiet. If we are to follow Jesus, we have to be free of financial concerns; we have to experience that life is great without an abundance of possessions.

When Jesus told people to sell their possessions, he was only partly telling them they should give to the poor; more than that, he was telling them to clear the decks for action. The idea was to travel light so that they'd be free to follow wherever he led.

And though he talked especially about money, that was not all he wanted us to be free of:

Those who come to me and do not hate their own father and mother and wife and children and brothers and sisters, yes, and even their own lives cannot be my disciples. (Luke 14:26)

Those who confront people like Marcos have to be prepared to be separated from more than their money; they may also be separated from their families, even from their lives.

To put it another way, money is a short leash; it keeps most of us at heel for our culture. In the West, governments and corporations do not need to threaten torture or even arrest. All they have to do is threaten our jobs, and we come to heel like Germans trotting after Hitler. (Meanwhile, because our leashes are made of dollars, we believe we live in a free society.)

Thomas Middleton makes a similar point in *Saturday Review*:

> There's an old maxim—or if there isn't there should be—that says, "If you want to corrupt a man, first make him rich." . . . Offering to make a man rich if he will compromise his principles might or might not work, depending largely upon the man's character. But take that same man and, without tempting him to betray himself, make him rich. Give him a couple of years to become accustomed to his house, his swimming pool, his tennis court, his Mercedes-Benz, and his golf club membership; then threaten to cut off the source of all the goodies. It will be as though you are threatening his very life. His dreary old principles will suddenly seem insignificant, and he will see things from a new angle, very close to that of Daddy Warbucks.[1]

But it does not seem to me that this leash works only with the rich. In my experience, laborers, teachers, ministers, writers— all of us become subservient when our jobs are at issue (especially if the job market is tight). We too are desperate to protect our houses (even if they are small), our cars (Plymouths this time), and our club memberships (the YMCA).

Possessions can easily control us, but not so easily if we travel light. Then we can become prophetic evangelists.

But what is prophetic evangelism?

It is evangelism that sounds more like Amos and Jesus than your average television evangelist. It understands our world to be in a struggle between darkness and light and calls people to serve the light. It calls people to love, justice, and peace. It understands the rich as oppressors who must repent and be forgiven or face justice to come. It understands the poor as people who must repent and be forgiven but one of the things they must repent of is kowtowing to the rich.

To be concrete, in some cases prophetic evangelism might look a lot like a Madison Square Gardens evangelistic rally. Except that violence, greed, and racism would be denounced as clearly as sexual promiscuity and drunkenness. And coming forward would signify not only a desire to be forgiven but a willingness to fight alongside the poor.

Personally, I'm partial to prophetic evangelism where you use your body to obstruct building a missile site. It is prophetic evangelism when you make a clear statement that the nation and its people must choose between serving the crucified God and the crucifying bomb.

Or prophetic evangelism might be a conversation over the back fence. Maybe you could talk to your neighbor about God and the poor or suggest that there's more to life than a new car and a secure income.

People need to be challenged to take stock of their lives. They need to explore whether they're hurting and oppressing others, whether they are committing suicide by wasting their lives, whether they are selling ice boxes on the burning deck. Then they need to be told of forgiveness through Christ's death—and of change through his resurrection.

But radical Christians are often hung up over evangelism. We'll vote, or we'll march in demonstrations, or we'll wear badges for Solidarity and the United Farm Workers. But we hesitate to say too much about God. And we're not about to ask people to decide whom they serve.

And that's understandable. After all, many of the most visible evangelists are franchising death. They do not point to springs of living water but to a fire escape from hell. Where they have flourished so have sexual repression, racism, legalized violence, and economic oppression (along with their own financial empires).

And even the saner advocates of evangelism have rarely understood the breadth of biblical evangelism. Or of today's problems. They have not seen the gospel's emphasis on the poor and oppressed, or the centrality it gives to rejecting financial idolatry. So they never ask rich young rulers to sell their possessions—or do anything else drastic. And they don't have a broad enough view of the gospel to call people to light their candles in the struggle against darkness and oppression.

In other words, the evangelism that we have seen often strengthens the very forces we oppose. It feeds rather than challenges the injustice and dehumanization of our day.

In good instances (and there are thousands), traditional evangelism helps people get their lives together. And that is not nothing. But it rarely produces a deep distress over racism or over official violence. And people who get their lives together without changing whom they serve, without becoming ready to be arrested—such people may be dangerous.

The main problem with traditional evangelism is its restricted idea of sin. Sin is understood only as things like adultery, lying, cheating, pornography, killing (when not in uniform), and stealing. You know the things people on television try not to do when the parson is around: swear, tell dirty jokes, drink. This list has some biblical roots, but it has more roots in what our culture disapproved of fifty years ago.

What is not on the list is especially striking. Whatever happened to oppression, greed, racism, failure to give to the poor, violence by officials, and taking advantage of the weak? Somehow traditional evangelists never see such things as sin. Adultery may be a sin, but racism is merely a misdemeanor.

Yet when the Bible deals with good and bad, its lists are remarkable for their breadth. Take Leviticus 19. It covers so much it's almost absurd. I don't know how to give a feel for its breadth except by actually listing what it discusses. So here goes: respect for parents, rest on the sabbath, idolatry, the proper use of sacrificial animals, leaving part of the harvest for poor people, stealing, cheating, lying, speaking falsely under oath, delaying the pay of laborers, cursing the deaf and tripping the blind, partiality in court, slander, taking vengeance and bearing grudges, loving your neighbor as yourself, mixing kinds of seed or cloth or cattle, sex with an unmarried slave, eating fruit from a tree less than five years old, eating meat with blood in it, witchcraft, sacred prostitution, mediums, respect for the elderly, wronging strangers, varied weights and measures, and a few others. When the Bible addresses morality, it covers the waterfront: idolatry, oppression, ecology, sex, witchcraft, love, justice.

Jeremiah is not quite so extravagant, but in a single sermon he denounces (among other things) adultery, idolatry, and oppression:

> When I fed them to the full,
>   they committed adultery
>   and trooped to the houses of harlots.
> They were well-fed, lusty stallions
>   each neighing for his neighbor's wife.
>
> The house of Israel and the house of Judah
>   have been utterly faithless to me, says the Lord.
>
> They set a trap;
>   they catch people.
> Like a basket full of birds,
>   their houses are full of treachery;
> therefore they have become great and rich,
>   they have grown fat and sleek.
> They judge not with justice
>   the cause of the fatherless. (Jer. 5:7, 8, 11, 26, 27, 28)

Jesus covers a similar range of subjects in the Sermon on the Mount (Matt. 5–7), the Sermon on the Plain (Luke 6), and in his extended attack on the scribes and Pharisees (Matt. 23). In the Sermon on the Mount he covers humility, mercy, persecution, letting your light shine, anger, lust, divorce, taking oaths, nonresistance, love, doing things for others to see, materialism, trusting God, judging others, and on and on and on.

Jesus and the Bible know no narrow list of sins; their conception of evil is broad and biting. And that's what makes evangelism prophetic.

Christians have endless debates about the relationship between evangelism and social action, and the debates never seem to lead anywhere. The idea of prophetic evangelism seems to me to give a way out of the debate—it refocuses the questions.

Prophetic evangelism is not the traditional liberal answer of collapsing social action and evangelism into one another. In liberalism doing good is about all that's left, and people are never asked to decide who their master is. Clearly, feeding the poor is a moral imperative, and it should encourage people to become Christians, but it certainly is not to be confused with repenting.

Nor does prophetic evangelism give a secondary place to social action like most approaches that emphasize the importance of evangelism. Paying the poor a decent wage is not an optional extra, nor is it something to be left for a mature stage of discipleship produced after years of teaching. No, it is an immediate moral necessity. Economic oppression is as serious as rape, and growing fat and sleek off Philippine bananas while Philippine kids starve is as bad as armed robbery. They are all sin. That is the central point of prophetic evangelism.

But that does not mean that all sin is removed from our lives the moment we choose a new master. Being converted is not like being struck by lightning. (The idea that it is produces instant converts who are like instant mashed potatoes—tasteless and terrible). Repentance and conversion are a continuing process; they are a lifelong vocation.

Finally, prophetic evangelism is not dualistic. Some progressive evangelicals stress that social action and evangelism are necessary but separate activities. Social action may prepare the way for more effective evangelism, and evangelism may prepare the way for increased social action, but the two are separate, at least conceptually. That is, a soup kitchen may soften up the poor to become Christians, and evangelism will produce more people to staff the soup kitchens, but the two activities are quite different. And, in my opinion, that's all true, as far as it goes.

However, prophetic evangelism connects social action and evangelism more integrally. From the perspective of prophetic evangelism, most of the world's problems are moral and spiritual; so the crucial thing is to call sinners to repentance. Poverty is largely the result of sin, especially oppression; so the solution is not soup kitchens but evangelizing oppressors. Third World hunger is indeed caused by drought, but it's not a drought of water; it's a drought of the word of God. So the most important kind of social action is evangelism.

Of course, the presidents of the Philippines and the United States aren't likely to repent, and neither are big landholders or boards of directors. (It's easier for a camel to get through the eye of a needle.) So we will need soup kitchens for a long time to come. But remember, such things don't deal with sin. They only alleviate its effects. Nonetheless, like Elijah bearding Ahab (1 Kings 21) or Jonah in Ninevah (Jonah 3), we must confront the oppressors. Sometimes, as in those two cases, prophetic evangelism works, producing change that is real and deep.

And then there is God. Prophetic evangelism deals with the spiritual as well as the moral. The struggle against enveloping darkness involves spiritual forces greater than ourselves. God and the prince of darkness are the key beings, and our relationship to them determines which side we're on. Reconciliation with God is at the heart of it all.

We are magnificent beings, made in the image of God. And we live in a wonderful, beautiful universe. God showed us a way of life centered on a deep relationship with God and all God's creation. Life could have been full of joy and peace and fun. But we would have none of it. We disrupted our relationship with God by doing dreadful things. We hurt others. We oppress them if they're weak. We get sucked into devoting vast sections of our lives to glittery things that use up the world God gave us. In short, we are busy spreading darkness for the prince of darkness. We do not serve God but mammon. We have turned our backs on our creator and are moving away from the center of our lives, leaving a trail of death and destruction and malignancy.

The way out is a restored relationship to God. This alone will restore our other relationships, our environment, our ethics, our politics. They are all of one piece.

Consider the Exodus. Was it sacred or secular? Was it a spiritual event or a political one? In liberation theology it was a secular event and little more; it was oppressed people fighting successfully for their political and economic rights. For politically conservative Christians, the Exodus was a spiritual event with little political or economic importance. But biblically, God and liberation are a package deal. Surely the Exodus was sacred, economic, political, moral, spiritual, and social. It was all those things at the same time.

But at the heart of it was God. Moses was not a self-appointed revolutionary leader. His commission came in an encounter with God, and without that spiritual encounter there would have been no liberation movement. When Moses went up to the burning bush, God told him to remove his shoes, for he was standing on holy ground (Exod. 3:5). And then what does the holy God do but start talking politics? Concern for justice in politics is part of God's holiness: "I have seen the affliction of my people, and I have heard their cry because of their taskmasters; I know their suffering, and I have come down to deliver them" (Exod. 3:7, 8). For the God of Israel, oppression is evil; opposing it is part of holiness.

The centrality of God in putting things right is emphasized again and again in the Exodus story. The liberation of Israel was the result of God's intervention. The core of Israel's ethics, the Ten Commandments, grew out of an encounter with God. And the foundation of the Law is the holiness of a compassionate God in liberating the Israelites from Egypt. It's all God-centered.

So the Ten Commandments begin, "I am the Lord your God who brought you out of the land of Egypt, out of the house of bondage" (Exod. 20:2). Individual laws are also connected to God. The law on lending to the poor ends, "If they cry to me, I will hear, for I am compassionate (Exod. 22:27). And Leviticus 19, part of the Holiness Code, begins this way: "You shall be holy, for I the Lord your God am holy" (v. 2). It ends: "I am the Lord your God who brought you out of the land of Egypt. And you shall observe all my statutes and all my ordinances and do them: I am the Lord" (vv. 36–37). The Holiness Code has a refrain: "I am the Lord." It occurs more than thirty times in ten chapters.

Among the Prophets the same God-centeredness is found. The Prophets are famous for their attacks on injustice, but they denounce turning from God every bit as often:

> My people have forsaken me,
> the fountain of living waters
>   and hewed out cisterns for themselves,
> broken cisterns,
>   that can hold no water. (Jer. 2:13)

The key to everything is restoring our relationship to God.

That is the key to prophetic evangelism.

Prophetic evangelism then means asking people to choose between two ways of life—serving God or serving the prince of darkness. We have chosen the wrong way, and such wickedness is not to be sneezed at. Sensitive people are sometimes haunted by things they've done, and they should be. But by God's grace, we can repent, be forgiven, and change. Our relationship to God and to others can be restored.

In America, prophetic evangelists will proclaim that we are

freed from the American dream: that is, we don't need to get rich, get laid, or get even. We don't need to kill poor and oppressed people just because the government tells us to. We don't need to eat food grown on land that should be feeding hungry people in the third world.

We are free at last.

God "has rescued us from the dominion of darkness and transferred us to the kingdom of the beloved son, in whom we have redemption and the forgiveness of sins" (Col. 1:13–14).

17. Structural Change or Cultural Revolution?

But how will my spending less and becoming a prophetic evangelist help José? How will that change the structures that are crushing him? Maybe New Testament evangelism was never intended to produce political and economic change.

Certainly Jesus didn't work at it the way people like me do. Things were every bit as bad under the Roman empire as they are under the American and Soviet empires. Yet Jesus didn't join the local guerrillas. Nor did he mount a nationwide, nonviolent campaign. He didn't organize unions, start co-ops, or paint "Yankee go home" on walls. He didn't even spend time denouncing the superpowers of his day the way I do denouncing the superpowers of my day.

He didn't back any particular structural change.

And that's a problem for people like me. You see, we talk all the time about following Jesus and then turn around and in the name of Jesus back specific economic and political structures. Which Jesus didn't do.

We think structures need to be changed. The reason kids starve is not shortage of food; there's plenty of food for all of us to eat. The reason kids starve is the economic system—the way food is distributed. Food goes to the highest bidder, and American cows can outbid Third World kids. Therefore American cows eat soybeans while Third World kids eat air. Now that's wrong; so people like me want to change the system of distribution.

What we believe in (besides Jesus) is structural change.

It's all very well to change individuals, but injustice is caused by sinful structures as well as by sinful individuals, and changing individuals doesn't immediately change structures. In the Old Testament getting individual kings to repent might have worked because the kings were more like oriental despots—they had absolute power. But if the president of the United States repented, that wouldn't necessarily change the structures much. He'd have centuries of law to correct, and he couldn't do it unless Congress repented, too. And even what he supposedly controls—for instance, the State Department and the Pentagon—might not follow his directives. Institutions have a life of their own.

Take, for example, a company moving to the South or the Third World so it can pay lower wages. Since companies exist mostly to make money, they will naturally move if it increases profits, and it makes little difference if the individual directors repent: moving is the logic of the institution. What's needed is structural change: perhaps worker-owned companies. Workers care about their own employment, so they won't move the company.

Or consider black beans in Brazil. There farmers used to grow black beans that poor people ate. However, farmers have learned that they can earn more by growing soybeans for American cows. So naturally Brazilian farmers grow soybeans, our cows eat the soybeans, and Brazilian kids eat air. Those Brazilian farmers probably aren't malicious; they are just making a sound business decision prompted by a vicious system. Getting them saved won't do much. What's needed is structural change: Perhaps Brazil should redistribute its land, putting it in the control of the people who need the black beans, and the United States should ban food imports from countries where people are starving.

A more complex case is the present urban housing crisis. Many middle-class people have decided that urban living has advantages over suburban living. They are moving back to the city, and naturally prices are skyrocketing. Naturally poor people can't even afford to live in the slums anymore. It's not mainly the result of a conspiracy of the wealthy. Nor are the buyers, bankers, or real estate agents necessarily malicious. The price inevitably rises when more people want to buy; this happens in systems where money controls distribution. Money controls who has decent housing, who eats, who has jobs—and within limits, even who lives. The trouble is the system of distribution. Changing that would be structural change. Such change might mean guaranteeing basic physical needs like housing, food, and medicine through an expanded welfare system.

Or it might mean redistributing wealth, or starting nongovernment housing co-ops and land trusts. It might mean making all housing the property of the state, which then assigned it by need. All of those would be structural change.

People like me are into things like that.

But Jesus doesn't seem to have been. He attacks the political and religious leaders of Israel and calls them to repentance—individually (Matt. 23). But he never suggests reorganizing the Sanhedrin or throwing the Romans out.

Does that mean Jesus kept out of politics? Was he only concerned about personal salvation? Were politics and justice Moses' and Amos' thing but not Jesus' and Paul's?

In my opinion, it is understandable to answer those questions with a yes, but it is also mistaken. I believe Jesus intended to change economic and political structures. Only he was doing it in a more profound way than we do.

Jesus does not propose any particular economic theory or sponsor any specific economic system. He does better than that. What he does is to condemn the profit motive and completely reject acquisitiveness. According to Jesus, the drive to make money is at best irrelevant and at worst destructive; what counts in this world is people, not things. Possessions and making money just aren't what life is about.

If such values were accepted, they would have revolutionary effects on economic structures. Our consumer society would stop dead in its tracks. There would be no one to buy the junk that our economic system pours out—and no one to make it, promote it, or retail it. The economy would turn more toward human services and human products: food, health maintenance, home care, education, family enrichment. And more money would be available for spiritual concerns and for the oppressed and the sick. Consumers would be transformed into servants, and the entrepreneurs and executives now driven by the desire for money or power would be freed to serve others. We would all find better things to do, and capitalism as we know it would be unthinkable. That was Jesus' approach.

What Jesus did was not to attack the machinery of capitalism and communism or their first century counterparts; instead he suggested unplugging the machinery. He suggested removing their source of power—greed. To change the metaphor, our way of fighting an octopus is to hack off the tentacles one at a time (or even to stick bubble gum in each suction cup), but Jesus' way was to cut its central nerve.

And that seems to be the usual approach to structural change in the New Testament. Paul does the same kind of thing with slavery. I wish he had attacked the institution of slavery, but he didn't. He didn't forbid slavery, as I would have done, but he made slavery unthinkable. He unleashed an idea that in time destroyed slavery. He taught that slaves are our brothers and sisters. And obviously you cannot enslave your brothers and sisters. So Paul wrote to Philemon telling him that he was getting back his slave forever, "no longer as a slave but more than a slave, as a beloved brother" (Philem. v. 16). And he told slavemasters to remember, "The one who is both their master and yours is in heaven and shows no partiality" (Eph. 6:9).

Jesus and Paul approached women's rights the same way. They lived in a society where women weren't even second-rate citizens; they were property only a step above cows. But Jesus and Paul did not fight for women's rights. What Jesus did was treat women with respect; for example, women traveled with him in a way that other rabbis would have found unthinkable. And Paul proclaimed the equality of women (usually): "There is neither Jew nor Greek, there is neither slave nor free, there is neither male nor female; for you are all one in Christ Jesus" (Gal. 3:28).

With those words Paul unleashed endless cultural revolution. Racism, slavery, and sexism were revealed as monstrous. They violate the deepest core of our being, and once that idea is let loose, it cannot be stopped.[1]

So perhaps the reason that Jesus and the New Testament say so little about structural change is that structural change doesn't go far enough; they won't settle for piecemeal reform like that. They want something deeper and wider; they want to undercut our whole culture and replace it with something new.

They want cultural revolution.

This sounds a lot like a countercultural view of social change. The way to change society is not to try to set the structures right. It is to become new people ourselves and then drop out of the more corrupt structures and form new ones. The new community of the church is to be a model pointing toward more human institutions. Gradually co-ops will replace supermarkets, churches sharing their resources will replace banks charging interest, communes will replace private and scarce housing, and executives serving money will become nurses serving the sick.

Capitalism will end not because it is made illegal or because businesspeople are shot but because people are no longer interested in consuming.

This countercultural view has a powerful appeal, at least to me. It removes the element of coercion central to most plans for social change, it doesn't increase the power of the state the way most left of center plans do, and it is in line with what Jesus and the apostles did.

The countercultural view is an old one. It strongly influenced the monastic movement and is the view held by Anabaptists. It has helped shape the radical Catholic left and radical evangelicals. And it was the view of the new left in the 1960s, whose members sought to transform America by becoming new people.

Only it hasn't worked out that way. The history of the Church is strewn with the wreckage of Christian communes, and the people who used to belong to the new left now belong to the New York Stock Exchange. Communes haven't solved the housing shortage, simple living hasn't halted consumerism, and the kingdom hasn't come.

A lot of reasons could be given for the failure. We are wary of evangelism and therefore have little ability to spread the word. Often our spiritual lives are as dead as other people's; so while we may have unplugged capitalist greed as the source of power in our lives, we haven't plugged into an alternative source of power. Love for people sometimes degenerates into harsh judgmentalism for people who don't agree with us (and that's most people).

So you could argue that all we have to do is try again, and this time do it right. But I think the problem is more serious than that. The countercultural view, as usually stated, doesn't take sin seriously enough. It expects more than is possible in a fallen world.

Communes fell apart because the "new" people in them were still sinners. Members of the new left joined the New York Stock Exchange because its tinsel still glittered to their fallen eyes.

But that's not surprising. All that it shows is that a counterculture approach can't produce utopia, can't usher in the kingdom. And surely we all knew that. Neither can gradual reform. Or armed revolution. Only God can do that.

The best that any approach can do is three steps forward and two back, and we shouldn't be surprised if it's four back. Until the kingdom comes, all we can hope for is to moderate evil. We can't end it.

The question then is not whether countercultures can end evil but whether they can moderate it. If they have some limited effect on social structures, we should be content and not require them to work a total transformation.

It's hard to measure such things, but without doubt burning

draft cards and refusing to enter the army affected the outcome of the war in Vietnam. In fact, the right sometimes blames the United States defeat on the protests of dropouts. Even minor things like "natural" food and blue jeans have had a minor impact. Of course, big business and *Glamor* magazine co-opted them, but improved food getting into supermarkets is an improvement even if fat cats get the profit. And blue jeans are cheaper and more sensible even if some poor souls pay a fortune to have a designer name on them.

And radical Christians have had an effect on the church far beyond their numbers. The growing concern in standard churches about hunger, justice, and nuclear war is partly inspired by radical Christians, and so is the increasing emphasis on closer ties between church members.

So a counterculture sometimes has an effect.

But is it Jesus' way? That's the real question. Not whether it's effective. The prophets weren't very effective, but that doesn't mean they were wrong. Amos and Jeremiah were total failures; they had no effect on the social structures of their day. But they were doing what needed to be done. So let's not be too concerned about whether the countercultural approach is effective. The main question is whether it's right, whether it's what Jesus would be doing.

Jesus didn't come with a blueprint for economic and political structures. His approach was more countercultural. He may have taken this approach because he didn't live in a democracy as we do and was therefore less responsible for the government's actions. Or it may have been because his followers were too few for them to be backing political programs at that point. But I doubt it.

I think it was because he wanted deeper change. Jesus wouldn't approve of our consumer society, but I doubt that he would propose laws to ban advertising. He'd gut the whole society by offering us better things to do.

At least when confronted by people who wanted importance

and power, he gutted the whole idea in much that way. He didn't discuss the dangers of having too much power or of wanting to be emperor; he gave us something better to do. He didn't tell the powerful to use their power responsibly to help the oppressed. Instead he proposed a radical alternative: He told people that being first just isn't worthwhile. Again and again he said, "The last shall be first and the first last" (Matt. 19:30; 20:16; Mark 9:35; Luke 13:30). And he told the disciples: "The kings of the gentiles lord it over them. But not so with you; rather let the greatest among you become as the youngest and the leader as one who serves" (Luke 22:25, 26). Jesus didn't want piecemeal improvements; he wanted total cultural revolution.

People who serve freely have a source of life that the world knows nothing about. They have a well of living water springing up inside.

Jesus' well of living water was clear at his trial. He wouldn't acknowledge Herod at all (Luke 23:8–9). He wouldn't even give him the time of day, let alone call on him to repent. The high priest and Pilate he answered when he felt like it, and not otherwise (Matt. 26:63; 27:12–14). His attitude was one of sublime contempt, a clear indication that he was not under their jurisdiction. His life was elsewhere.

After all, Jesus' kingdom is not of this world. He and his followers are rooted in a deeper reality that makes this one seem pale by comparison. In C. S. Lewis's *The Silver Chair*, as people watch the king meet the crown prince, Aslan appears "so bright and real and strong that everything else began at once to look pale and shadowy compared with him."[2] The reality of Jesus makes the rest of the world seem tinny and insignificant.

Does that mean that Christians should avoid working for specific laws? Should we stay out of the programmatic side of justice while painting pictures of the peaceable kingdom and inviting all to join? Going beyond that seems to me to be going beyond Jesus and the New Testament.

But perhaps I'm being naive. (Most Christians would certainly think so.) Perhaps what I'm doing is like arguing that Jesus didn't ride in cars and so we shouldn't either. Maybe I want Jesus and the New Testament to give me detailed recipes on how to live, and they never set out to do that.

Maybe Christians confronting injustice are like doctors confronting cancer. Jesus and the New Testament don't tell us what therapy to use for cancer, but they do tell us to relieve suffering. So doctors use their own judgment on what therapy will best relieve suffering. And why shouldn't we do the same thing with injustice? If a piece of legislation looks like it will relieve suffering, then not supporting it would be negligent.

Most often I think Jesus gave us fundamental principles and left it to us to construct the detailed blueprints. He gave us clues, a mindset. And we should fight structures that use different clues, that reflect a different mindset. And we should support those structures that strive to reflect the mind of Christ.

Let me put it differently. People with deeply held moral convictions apply them to all of life, including political and moral structures. I don't see how you can avoid it. Even those most adamant about separating politics and religion have always freely mixed them when it got to things they really cared about. So fundamentalists campaigned for prohibition (some evangelical areas are still dry), against pornography and prostitution, for prayer in public schools, and against homosexual rights, the Equal Rights Amendment, and abortion.

Convictions don't stay in compartments, and they shouldn't. People live out their beliefs in their whole lives. When they don't, it's because they don't really believe them. So people who say that "just structures" are not the concern of religion are most often people who don't care about "just structures." And, in my observation, those who say the government needn't turn the other cheek most often don't really believe individuals should either.

The point is that an idea planted bears fruit. And Jesus knew that. Jesus and Paul planted the idea that slaves were equal to their masters and women equal to men, and it was only a matter of time till their followers devised laws banning slavery and limiting discrimination against women. Those laws were inevitable results of rejecting the spirit of the age in favor of a new one. The seed Jesus planted produces new structures as it grows.[3]

Jesus gave us glimpses of a new vision of society, and our politics must be guided by those glimpses. It is left to us to draw the blueprints, but Jesus' vision of justice and love and peace and equality is the foundation.

And yet I am nervous. I am enough of a fundamentalist that I worry about promoting blueprints Jesus didn't draw.

For one thing, we're liable to confuse our blueprints with Jesus' vision and take them altogether too seriously. To talk of love and justice while avoiding applying them in relation to specific laws seems odd to me, but it would be wrong to suppose that the applications we make are the right ones and the only right ones. Our blueprints and Jesus' vision are on a very different level, and we must hang loose with our blueprints. We must keep a critical distance from them—a distance we don't keep from love and justice.

Even more important is keeping our priorities straight. Working for just laws has an important place, but it is not in the same league as living and proclaiming the gospel of the kingdom. The programmatic side of politics decidedly takes second fiddle to entering the kingdom yourself and inviting others to join you.

I have seen too many Christians (including myself half the time) get drawn into politics till they lose their spiritual roots. We get "up to our steeples in politics"[4] and have no time for nurturing the seeds that produce cultural revolution. Soon we forget that political problems are spiritual and moral, and that our basic task is to address them in moral and spiritual terms.

We lobby our congresspeople to vote to help the poor, but

somehow we never get around to inviting congresspeople or anyone else to repent and enter the kingdom. We work to improve the quality of life of the poor even when the quality of our own lives is degenerating in the process. We decide to be silent about consumerism in the hope of being taken more seriously about racism; but that's a trade-off Jesus never would have made, for he would have known that at root they are the same problem.

The priority of our spiritual vision has a counterpart of sorts in secular thinking: Dreams are more important than the details of legislation, ideas are more important than missiles. So in the continuing struggle between the United States and the Soviet Union, missiles matter less than blue jeans and rock music. As long as Soviet kids love blue jeans and American rock, the United States is winning those kids' hearts and minds no matter how many missiles the Soviet government builds.

By the same token, the strongest weapon the Soviets have is not the bomb; it is the promise of justice. As long as Third World people believe that promise, the Soviets are winning their hearts and minds whether justice is delivered or not. And all the American tanks and military advisers in the world won't change that.

Take Vietnam. I suspect that the reason the United States lost that war was not the superiority of guerrilla tactics. (If that were it, South Vietnam could have launched a guerrilla war after their defeat.) No, the United States lost because of the superiority of the guerrillas' ideas. The Vietnamese dream of national freedom and the Marxist dream of ending poverty overpowered the American dream tarnished by corrupt, puppet governments and tiger cages.

Of course, dreams do not always win—at least not right off. Estonia, Chile, Poland, and South Africa prove that. If politicians and soldiers are strong enough and ruthless enough, they can postpone dreams indefinitely—and occasionally even kill them. But in the long run, ideas generally win. ("The pen is mightier than the sword" and all that.)

That is why it is so crucial for Christians to focus on the ideas and dreams rather than using themselves up on the blueprints. Jesus brought the best dreams and visions: the hungry are fed, the insensitive rich are brought low, people are freed from the hypnotic power of possessions, executives become nurses.

If we want justice and peace, we must sell that dream. We must persuade people to choose Jesus' ideas and reject the spirit of the age. In short, we must evangelize.

Evangelization is the only hope for cultural revolution.

Let's be clear. We need changed people.

Sometimes we imagine that what we need is a fistful of new laws that will enforce justice and redistribute wealth. And that would certainly help.

But that solution suggests that the problem is a technical one—that we somehow haven't got around to passing the right laws. And that isn't true. The problem is sin. We don't have the right laws because we're too sinful to make the right laws. We serve a different kingdom.

So we need more than new laws. First, we need new people, people who will work for new laws, people who have been evangelized. If these new people succeed in passing new laws, the change won't be merely technical. It will be a moral and spiritual change. It will be a sign that more people are entering the kingdom and that the spirit of the age is being beaten back.

The same thing is true of politicians. We need new and better politicians, of course, but we shouldn't blame the politicians. We should blame the people who tolerate them. People have the politicians they deserve. Only brutal and insensitive people elect brutal and insensitive politicians. "The prophets prophesy falsely, and my people love to have it so" (Jer. 5:31).

The reason forty thousand poor kids die each day has little to do with politicians; it's that voters don't much care. So presidents standing for reelection when the economy is booming would be reelected even if they planned to starve all the kids in the Third World. But believe you me, if voters wouldn't tolerate kids dying, the politicians would find ways to take care of them.

My point is that a nation's laws and politicians reflect the spiritual state of that nation (at least in a democracy). Organizing and informing people can have some effect; it can at least counteract the influence of the moneyed special interests. (So political lobbies have a real, if limited, role.) But you can never raise the laws or the politicians much higher than the spiritual state of the people. Structures have to be changed as well as individuals, but you can't improve structures much without improving the people's spiritual state.

And we must improve our own spiritual state. Who we are finally outweighs what we do and say. How else are we to account for the way Jesus and Paul emphasized personal transformation while nearly ignoring structural change? Apparently they thought our personal state was the foundation of everything else.

Sometimes we campaign to save the environment while we ourselves are consumed by the spirit of consumerism. And that is hollow. And so are peace groups racked by internal hatred. They may unwittingly be doing more for the spirit of war than for the spirit of peace. Working for peace, justice, and compassion is crucial, but we must also live peace, justice, and compassion. Otherwise, we are being as hypocritical as the Pharisees.

I do not mean that in areas where we have personal failures we should remain silent about structures. We'll never have perfect personal lives; so we can't wait till we do. But we must oppose sin in ourselves as fiercely as we oppose sin in structures. To say the least, it is ironic to protest things in society which we tolerate in our own lives.

After all, our personal sins reinforce structural evil. I picture it this way: Our world is in such a mess because it has been captured by evil principalities and powers. It is in the thrall of the spirit of consumerism, the spirit of war, the spirit of racial superiority. Those spirits take form in economic and political structures, and they also take form in our lives. If we serve them personally, then we are feeding their fires no matter how firmly we denounce them in their structural forms. (By the same token, if we serve fallen structures, then we are feeding their fires even if we are free of them in our personal lives.)

We all have evil fires burning within us, and that contributes to the power of the conflagration in evil structures. Carrying a sign protesting a fire in a structure is good, but if the same fire is blazing unchallenged within, I wonder if it doesn't ignite the sign in our hands, adding fuel to the fire.

The problem is that we Christian political activists are liable to ignore the quality of our own lives, and that is tragic. Christian activists claim that society is violent, capitalistic, and racist. We call people to be rooted in a deeper reality, in the reality of the spring of living water. That way people won't need to kill, consume, and act as if they're better than people of a different color. They won't try to fill the hollow space inside themselves with such trash because it will already be filled by God.

But we can hardly tell people those things if we ourselves are hollow inside. We have to spend time on our own spiritual state, or we will have no political message at all.

For the spiritual is central in politics as in everything else. It is the foundation of the cultural revolution.

5. THE USES OF WEAKNESS

18. A Question of Class

The problem is that the dark fires of evil have an enormous attraction. Love and justice and truth are far superior to possessions and revenge and holocaust, but they don't have the same lure. The glitter of wealth and the dream of controlling or impressing others can make love look platitudinous.

The oppressed may dream of justice, but those on top have other dreams. Their dreams may be nothing worse than a lawn without crabgrass, but that is a terrible dream when it takes our attention away from forty thousand kids dying. So people do not combat evil; they combat crabgrass.

The problem, of course, is sin. The malign part of our nature is drawn by the glamor of evil. How do we fight such a terrible force?

We fight, I think, by weakness. Counterforce and power are irrelevant before such a juggernaut. God crucified in weakness and vulnerability is what halts evil.

But rather than attempt to dampen the fires of evil in the way Jesus modeled for us on the cross, people of goodwill try to enlist the rich and powerful and famous. We want the rich to finance the battle, the famous to give it recognition and credibility, the powerful to get things done.

And that's a sensible, natural way to proceed.

But I believe that instead of dampening the fires of evil, this approach makes them blaze brighter. For at the heart of evil is the whole system of money and power and status. To try to use them against evil merely reinforces the evil system. What we need to do instead is to enlist the poor, the weak, and the nobodies.

At least that's what Jesus did. That's the upside-down way

of the kingdom. To try to fight evil with money and power and reputation is like trying to fight fire with gasoline.

But I'm getting ahead of myself again.

It's a class question, at least in part. You defeat evil not by becoming part of the upper class or by getting the upper class to join the cause; you defeat evil by becoming part of the lower class, by persuading the lower class to enter the kingdom. Members of the upper class just aren't willing to enter the kingdom. They don't want to become lower class, to give away all, to become servants of all—toilet cleaners. But to the lower class, it's no big deal. They're already doing it.

Everyone knows how Jesus berated the Pharisees and chief priests—the ruling class. And we know how he spent his time with prostitutes, tax collectors, lepers—the lower class in Israel. But we rarely notice the class dimensions of all that.

This class consciousness appears in all the Gospels, though to varying degrees. All of them portray Israel's ruling class as being utterly opposed to Jesus, and all of them portray Jesus as having a strong following among the people. The Pharisees despised the people, the unruly mob, but the unruly mob "hung upon his words" (Luke 19:48).

This picture of a struggle between the classes is presented most consistently in Matthew. Matthew is almost built around this conflict. It began even before Jesus' ministry. Crowds came to John the Baptist, but when the Pharisees and Sadducees came, Matthew says he called them a "brood of vipers" (3:7; see also 21:26). So the stage was set for class conflict before Jesus made a public appearance.

Throughout Jesus' ministry the people flocked to him, common people who didn't even know the law and were too poor to keep ritual requirements.[1] They were the ones Jesus preached to and healed and fed: "When he saw the crowds, he had compassion on them, because they were harassed and helpless, like sheep without a shepherd" (9:36).

But the leaders of Israel, the establishment, were another

matter. The scribes and Pharisees were always attacking Jesus, and if they weren't, then it was the turn of the chief priests and elders of the people, or of the lawyers and the Levites. With only a handful of exceptions, the ruling class was utterly opposed to Jesus. They spent as much time criticizing him as the people did mobbing him. An amazing proportion of Matthew's gospel is devoted to the charges and countercharges between Jesus and the Pharisees.[2]

The typical attitude of the establishment is shown when "the Pharisees went and took counsel how to entangle him in his talk" (Matt. 22:15). But we get a different picture of the people:

Great crowds came to him, bringing with them the lame, the maimed, the blind, the dumb, and many others, and they put them at his feet and he healed them, so that the throng wondered when they saw the dumb speaking, the maimed whole, the lame walking, and the blind seeing; and they glorified the God of Israel. (15:30–31)

Matthew's first report of the contrasting attitude of the crowd and the rulers is when Jesus healed a paralytic by forgiving his sins. At that point the scribes accused him of blasphemy (9:3), but "when the crowds saw it, they were afraid and glorified God" (9:8). Then a few verses later Jesus cast out a demon. "The crowds marveled, but the Pharisees said, 'He casts out demons by the prince of demons' " (9:33, 34).

At the triumphal entry, things reached the boiling point:

Most of the crowd spread their garments on the road, and others cut branches from the trees and spread them on the road. And the crowds that went before him shouted, "Hosanna to the son of David! Blessed is he who comes in the name of the Lord! Hosanna in the highest!" And when he entered Jerusalem, all the city was stirred, saying, "Who is this?" And the crowds said, "This is the prophet Jesus from Nazareth of Galilee." And the blind and the lame came to him in the temple, and he healed them. But when the chief priests and the scribes saw the wonderful things that he did, and the children crying out in the temple, "Hosanna to the son of David!" they were indignant. (21:8–11, 14–15)

Crowds, the blind, the lame, and children were on one side, and on the other side were the chief priests and scribes.

The next day, Jesus told a series of parables admonishing the chief priests and scribes. Naturally they were enraged, "but when they tried to arrest him they feared the multitudes because these people held him to be a prophet" (21:46). When the authorities decided to have Jesus executed, they didn't dare do it openly (26:55). They decided "to arrest Jesus by stealth and kill him. But they said, 'Not during the feast, lest there be a tumult among the people' " (Matt. 26:4, 5).

According to Matthew the crucifixion reflected class conflict. The crowds mobbed him and glorified God for his works, but the establishment blasphemed and had him crucified. There is something about riches and power and respectability that blinds the eyes and hardens the heart. And there is something about poverty and weakness that leaves a person hungering and seeking.

> Blessed are you poor.
> Woe to you rich.

Perhaps even more significant than the two groups' contrasting response to Jesus is Jesus' contrasting response to them. He had compassion on the crowds, feeding them when they got hungry, and healing their sick, but he bitterly denounced the Jewish establishment. His rudeness to them is legend. He calls them a brood of vipers (Matt. 12:34; 23:33), an evil and adulterous generation (Matt. 12:39; 16:4), hypocrites (Matt. 15:7; 22:18; 23:13, 15, 25, 26, 27, 29; Mark 7:6; Luke 13:15), blind (Matt. 23:16, 17, 19, 24, 26), and fools (Matt. 23:17; Luke 11:40). The blistering he gave them in Matthew 23 makes modern yellow journalism look restrained:

> Woe to you, scribes and Pharisees, hypocrites! for you are like whitewashed tombs, which outwardly appear beautiful but inside are full of dead men's bones and all uncleanness. So you also outwardly appear righteous to people, but inside you are full of hypocrisy and inequity. (vv. 22–23)

Jesus did not exactly court the power brokers.

It's true that in Luke, Jesus banqueted with the Pharisees, but it is equally true that in every single instance he blasted them unmercifully (Luke 7:36–50; 11:37–52; 14:1–24). At one dinner party, Jesus was so rude to the Pharisees that a lawyer protested, "In talking this way, you reproach us, too" (Luke 11:45). And what did Jesus do? Did he duck it as any sensible person would? No, he said, "Woe to you lawyers, too!" (v. 46).

Meanwhile he was out being nice to the crowds. He seemed to actively go after people of the wrong sort. You know the list. He practically collected the blind, the lame, Samaritans, women, occasional gentiles, poor people, tax collectors, children, prostitutes, lepers—all sorts of riffraff. And he was hardly ever rude or abusive to them (never in Matthew or Mark; in John he gets close in 6:25–27; in Luke he speaks strong words in 11:29–32 and 12:54–56).

Clearly his approach to class was upside down. He alienated power brokers and opinion molders while courting outcasts.

Not that even Matthew sees the crowd as all good or the establishment as all bad. Matthew records the faith of a ruler of the synagogue in Galilee whose daughter Jesus raised from the dead (9:18–26). He also reports how Jesus' burial was arranged by a "rich man from Arimathea, named Joseph, who was also a disciple of Jesus" (27:57–60). And Jesus spoke to the crowd in parables because "to them it has not been given" to know the secrets of the kingdom (13:11). And at the triumphal entry, the crowds cheered Jesus, but they saw him as a prophet from Galilee, not as the messiah (21:11). That, of course, was a lot higher than the understanding the chief priests had of him, but it's low enough that the high priests could soon get some of this beloved, unruly crowd howling for his crucifixion (26:47, 55; 27:20–26).

But it was the chief priests who whipped them up. The crucifixion was not the crowd's idea; it was the establishment's. According to Matthew, it was the upper class, the rulers, who had Jesus crucified.

The picture in the other gospels is not as clear, but it comes to nearly the same thing. They are more critical of the crowds and less devoted to attacking the Pharisees.

Power killed him. Weakness followed him.

It was a question of class.

Luke puts more emphasis on class than any other book in the Bible.

Luke starts with the announcement of John the Baptist's birth. It is no accident that his mother had been barren. Like Sarah and Hannah before her, she felt disgraced by having no child, but God finally removed her reproach (1:25). That is the kind of God Jehovah is.

The next story Luke tells is of the angel appearing to Mary to announce the birth of Jesus. God is being born—but not into a powerful or wealthy family. God picks a humble girl, probably about sixteen. Mary herself thought that she was nobody and talked about "the low estate of God's handmaiden" (1:48).

For, according to Luke, God chooses to use people of low estate, people like Elizabeth and Mary. In fact, this practice seems to be a theological principle:

> God has scattered the proud in the imagination of their hearts,
> God has put down the mighty from their thrones
> and exalted those of low degree;
> God has filled the hungry with good things
> and sent the rich empty away. (1:51, 52–53)

The most amazing thing about these verses is their absolute nature. They flatly assert that the mighty are going to be smashed and the lowly raised up. There are no restrictions—no ifs, ands, or excepts. The mighty are offered no escape clauses for being good, nor are the lowly warned that they will be lifted up only if they behave. No, God rejects the rulers (the upper class) in favor of the poor (the lower class).

Chapter 2 continues the theme: God was not born in a palace or a mansion; he was not born in Rome or even in Jerusalem. He was born in a manger in Bethlehem. The Holiday Inn was full, and Joseph and Mary weren't important enough to pull strings to get in; so Jesus was born in an old garage out back. The birth announcement was made by angels, which is pretty classy, but they didn't make it to Herod or the Sanhedrin or anyone like that. They made it to shepherds—infamous thieves.

Later Mary and Joseph took Jesus to the temple for the purification ceremony, and they were too poor to afford the normal offering (Luke 2:24).[3] So Jesus was born into a home that was dirt poor.

In Luke 3 John the Baptist's class consciousness is clear. He was concerned about the poor and called for a radical response. Those with two coats, if they repented, were to give one of them to someone with none.

Luke 4 reports Jesus' first sermon, and the social message is the usual: "The Spirit . . . has sent me to proclaim release to the captives and recovering of sight to the blind, to set at liberty those who are oppressed" (4:18). Jesus considered himself called to minister to the suffering, to the lower class. His mission was not for those at ease.

But the really striking line is often neglected: The Spirit "has anointed me to preach good news to the poor" (4:18). Jesus didn't just say he was anointed to preach good news, nor did he say he was anointed to preach good news to everyone. It blows my mind, but he said he was anointed to preach *to the poor*. The middle class and the upper class did not even get a mention.

The rest of Luke 4, most of Luke 5, and the beginning of Luke 6 tell of Jesus casting out demons and healing the sick. Meanwhile fishermen and a tax collector followed him, and the Pharisees got upset because of the class of people Jesus was associating with (6:30).

The nobodies flocked to Jesus, but the ruling class was entrenched against him.

It was a question of class.

Surely everyone is equal before God. It's true that the poor are every bit as good as the rich, but by the same token aren't the rich every bit as good as the poor? "We hold these truths to be self-evident: all men are created equal. . . ." Surely God isn't going to discriminate against people just because they are rich or intelligent or powerful.

No, I don't suppose God will.

But maybe the rich will discriminate against God. Maybe the rich and beautiful and clever don't know they need God. Maybe only people in trouble seek God—maybe people have to be in foxholes to seek God. Maybe riches and power harden peoples' hearts to God and to the suffering of others. Then God can't get through to them.

If so, woe to the rich.

It's a question of class.

Remember the prodigal son and his brother? (Luke 15:11–32). The prodigal son felt no need of his father until he had made a mess of his life. Then he went back home. As long as he was prospering, he was self-sufficient, or at least he thought he was.

Maybe that's what the rich think.

And the brother? The one who hadn't made a mess of his life? He was angry, unforgiving, and unloving. He was the sort who saw no need to help prodigals, no need for forgiveness, no need for God. He was rich.

And what about the two men who went to the temple to pray, one a Pharisee and the other a tax collector? Not that either of them was necessarily rich, but the tax collector had the attitude typical of the poor and the Pharisee had the attitude typical of the rich. "God be merciful to me a sinner" is the attitude of a poor person who has made a mess, and "God, I thank you that I am not like others, not like this tax collector" is the attitude of the rich who have life down pat.

It's a question of class.

But what does it all mean?

It means that the rich and the strong don't often enter the kingdom. They are too self-reliant. It means that the poor and the messed up are more likely to enter the kingdom. They sense their need for God.

It doesn't mean that the rich never enter the kingdom or that the poor always do. Some rich people are humble enough, broken enough, to enter. And some poor people are too proud and self-reliant to enter.

It does mean that you can talk about the rich and the poor as classes whose typical responses are different. Sometimes that may seem like overgeneralizing, but the Bible does it. (Hyperbole must be a Christian way to talk.)

But more important, it gives us some clues on how to fight the fires of evil. In that battle we don't court the Sanhedrin or try to get the emperor's family on our side. (They probably wouldn't join us anyway, and if they did, it might mean we were doing something wrong.) The people we need as allies are the poor and oppressed, the ignorant and the handicapped. Getting them on our side dampens the fires.

I often see advertising for books and magazines that say things like, "Required reading in the U.S. Senate" or "The president's favorite magazine." But I think a more Christian recommendation would be, "The president and most senators hate this magazine, but it is read avidly by Rosie the waitress, George the truck driver, and Maggie the streetwalker with venereal disease."

Now when that begins happening, the fires of evil will burn less brightly.

19. The Imitation of Christ

Why didn't Jesus come as the Roman emperor? That is a crucial question facing the church today. Why didn't Jesus come in power?

Jesus could have come as the emperor, but no, he thought carpentry would be a better profession. Now I ask you, what use is carpentry to a messiah? Think what Jesus could have done as the emperor. He could have given an order, and a soldier would have been standing on every street corner in the empire, saying "Repent, for the kingdom of heaven is at hand." Or he could have erected marble pillars all over the empire, inscribed with things like "Blessed are the meek," "Sell your possessions."

Why did he wait three hundred years for Constantine? As an emperor he could have spread the word so much more quickly and thoroughly than as a carpenter. People take emperors seriously; they can't just ignore them the way they can a laborer. With an emperor's connections. . . .

And anyone knows that reform goes easier if you've got the local Sanhedrin on your side; so I'd have gone a long way out of my way to keep the bigwigs happy. The endorsement of a few Pharisees and Sadducees would have been just what we wanted. If a Nicodemus had once come to us, we'd have urged him to appear on the platform with us. But no, Jesus didn't do it that way. He made no effort to line up the big wheels. If he tried to line anyone up, it was the riffraff—lepers, poor people, and prostitutes.

As for his disciples, they were not exactly riffraff, but they certainly were not a high-powered sponsoring committee. A tax collector, a revolutionary, several middle-class fishermen—people of that sort. No rich people, no nobility, no one from Harvard Law School, no Olympic athletes, not even a doctor or a runner-up for Miss America. I don't know about you, but I'd want better backing than that.

It's as if the messiah were an Indian from some mountain village in Central America, and his more respectable followers were Indian shopkeepers. How do you think that would go over in New York or Washington? Especially if the ambassador hadn't met him, and no one from Congress or the house of bishops appeared on the same platform with him?

No, the gospel comes in weakness.

It has to be that way.

But perhaps the fact that Jesus came in weakness has no bearing on how we should lead our lives. Perhaps the fact that Jesus did not seek the endorsement of the beautiful people tells us nothing about how we should work for social change. Perhaps when Jesus said, "Follow me," he did not mean for us to imitate his life; perhaps he only meant for the people of his own day to join the group that traveled with him.

For many Christians the only part of Jesus' life that counts is his death, and what counts about that is that it was for our sins. They do not think that the way Jesus lived and died is intended to show us the path to life. For these people, Jesus' death is central because in his death Jesus atoned for our sins; but his life has no centrality morally, no special role as a model for living.

From that point of view, the only objection to Jesus' coming as the Roman emperor is that it wouldn't have fulfilled prophecy. And the only need for the incarnation is to show that some human being could lead a sinless life. So, from that point of view God could almost have come to earth just for a short time to be tortured for our sins and need not have bothered to be born or to have lived a human life at all.

But the imitation of Jesus is a theme that runs throughout the New Testament. According to repeated biblical teaching, we are to follow him.

This theme is obvious in the Gospels where Jesus calls people to follow him. Some of the passages are calls to specific people to join his wandering band, and those have little importance to us. Thus his call to Peter and Andrew (Matt. 4:18–20; Mark 1:16–18; Luke 5:1–11) is not a call for us to follow Jesus. (It may, however, be indicative of our call, as suggested in the mass of sermons on becoming "fishers of men.")

But sometimes Jesus calls all to follow him: "Those who do not take up their cross and follow me are not worthy of me" (Matt. 10:38; see also Luke 14:27; Matt. 16:24; Mark 8:34; Luke 9:23). John's Gospel contains several equally universal sayings. "Anyone who serves me must follow me" (John 12:26). "I am the light of the world; those who follow me will not walk in darkness but will have the light of life" (8:12). "The sheep follow the shepherd for they know his voice. A stranger they will not follow" (10:4–5). "My sheep hear my voice, and I know them, and they follow me" (10:27). These passages indicate that we are to live the same sort of life that Jesus led.

In several other places the Gospels make the same point but without using the words "Follow me." For example, in Luke 6:40 Jesus says, "Disciples are not above their teacher, but all disciples when they are fully taught will be like their teacher." And Matthew has a similar saying, "It is enough for disciples to be like their teacher, and servants like their master" (10:25).

After washing the disciples' feet, Jesus says, "For I have given you an example, that you should do as I have done to you" (John 13:15). And when the disciples squabbled over who would be greatest, Jesus told them that the fact that he himself served showed them how to live (Mark 10:44; Matt. 20:28; Luke 22:27).

We are to be like Jesus.

But in what ways should we imitate Jesus? Should we wear sandals and have long hair? Should we ride on donkeys?

Obviously not. We are to imitate him only in morally relevant respects. But there's the rub. Which respects are morally relevant?

In a general way, the answer is clear enough. We should be loving and honest, we should care for the hurting, and we shouldn't kill, for example.

Ah . . . but already we are in trouble. Clearly we shouldn't commit murder, but how about resisting unjust arrest? Why didn't Jesus and the disciples fight the soldiers who came to get him? Was it because he wanted to teach us nonviolence, or was it because he had a special mission we don't have—to atone for our sins? In other circumstances would he have fought? How do we know which parts of Jesus' life were meant as examples and which were historical accidents?

I don't believe for a moment that the fact that Jesus was born in a stable means that the maternity wards of Christian hospitals should use mangers for babies' beds. Nor do I believe that his virgin birth means that Christians should try to have children without sex. But I do believe, for instance, that Jesus' practice of having next to no possessions was intended as an example for us. I suspect that it is no accident that we are never told things like his eye color, the length of his hair, or the color of his robe. If we were, some people would be bound to cut their hair his length or idealize people with eyes his color. What the text emphasizes is things like the sort of people Jesus worked with, the way he gave his life, the ways he helped people, his humble origins and way of life.

Jesus didn't teach much on hair length or eye color, and so we needn't imitate him in those respects. But he did teach about poverty and wealth, so we should look to his life to see how he fleshed out his teachings. And with any subject he taught on, we can properly look to his life for guidance on what he meant.

Passages which tell us to follow Jesus link that to his poverty, his weakness, his suffering and death. We are to start on a downward journey that may end in crucifixion. That is how we are to imitate him.

Philippians says it all:

In humility count others as better than yourselves. Let each of you look not only to your own interests, but also to the interests of others. Have this mind among yourselves, which is yours in Christ Jesus, who, though he was in the form of God, did not count equality with God a thing to be grasped, but emptied himself, taking the form of a servant, being born in human likeness. And being found in human form he humbled himself and became obedient unto death, even death on the cross. (Phil. 2:3, 4–8)

Jesus Christ was on the top of the heap, but he went to the bottom. He was God, but he became weak and poor, a suffering servant who was tortured. That is how we are to imitate him.

Almost all the passages about following Jesus are saying that. To be specific, a good many of them teach leaving family and possessions. That's part of the downward journey. The individual calls to disciples resulted in their leaving their nets, their boats, their fathers—everything (Matt. 4:20, 22; Luke 5:11, 28). That is also precisely what Jesus asked of the scribe who wanted to follow him and of the disciple who wanted to bury his father. It is also precisely what Jesus had done himself: he had left his wealth and his father, and they were called to do the same. When Jesus called the rich young ruler to follow him, he called him to give up his possessions—as Jesus had already done (Matt. 19:21). And Paul makes the imitation theme explicit in relation to possessions. When he urged the Corinthians to give to the church at Jerusalem, the reason he gave was that Jesus had done that sort of thing (2 Cor. 8:9).

But the vast majority of verses about following Jesus ask even more. They are calling us not only to leave family and possessions but also to give up our lives. We are to become suffering servants like Jesus. John 13:15, after the footwashing, stresses servanthood: "For I have given you an example, that you should do as I have done to you."

Other passages understand serving in even more drastic terms: They call us to be crucified. In a whole array of sayings, Jesus links following him with being crucified:

All who would come after me, let them deny themselves and take up their crosses daily and follow me. For those who would save their lives will lose them, and those who lose their lives for my sake will save them. (Luke 9:23–24; see also Matt. 6:23; Mark 8:34)

Just before that statement, Jesus warned his disciples that he was about to be executed (Luke 9:22). So "take up your cross" is not an airy-fairy statement about wearing a gold religious symbol in your lapel. He was talking about a wooden cross where you sweat and bleed and die. That's what imitating Jesus means.

The first three Gospels all record James' and John's efforts to be named the most important people in the kingdom. Jesus' answer weaves together being a servant and dying—or rather it says that true service may lead to death, not to the kind of glory James and John had in mind:

You know that those who are supposed to rule over the Gentiles lord it over them, and their great men exercise authority over them. But it shall not be so among you; whoever would be great among you must be your servant, and whoever would be first among you must be slave of all. For the Son of man also came not to be served but to serve and to give his life as a ransom for many. (Mark 10:42, 43–45; see also Matt. 20:28; Luke 22:27)

Those who follow the Son of man are servants even unto death.

This point is made clearly in the moving story at the end of the book of John (John 21:15–23) where Peter is twice told to follow Jesus. At an earlier time, he had been told the same thing, and he had left his boat to follow Jesus. But now he was back fishing, discouraged and crushed. His Lord had been crucified, and before that Peter had denied him three times. So

once more Jesus came to the Sea of Galilee to talk to the fisher-
man. Three times Jesus asked if Peter loved him, three times
Jesus told him to feed his sheep, and then he twice repeated
the old call, "Follow me."

Apparently he was calling Peter to die. Peter's fear, which
had prompted him to deny Jesus, had been that he too might
be arrested and maybe even killed. And Jesus was telling him
that he was right: He must follow the one who was crucified.
And, in an apparent reference to crucifixion, Jesus even told
him that he would stretch out his hands. But Peter's eyes fell
on John, and he asked, "Ah, but what about him? How will he
die?" And Jesus said, "What business is that of yours? Your
only job is to follow me" (John 21:22).

And on that note the Gospel of John ends. Following Jesus
means following Jesus to the cross. And that is the way to put
out the fires of evil.

20. Crucifixion

Crucifixion was a Roman way of torturing people to death. In public. Slowly.

The victim was generally a slave or someone resisting Roman rule. First he was scourged. Whipped until his back was raw meat: That helped him feel the cross on his back. Then he was forced to take up his own cross and carry it to the place of crucifixion. There he was tied or nailed to the cross, naked, and the cross was lifted up and set in the earth. Death came from exhaustion, from gradual suffocation, when the victim could no longer hold up enough of his weight to let himself breathe. The Romans provided a wooden block on which the victim "sat." The block meant he could hold up his weight longer—and die more slowly. Sometimes it took a couple of days.

It was not a nice way to die. That was the idea. The Romans wanted people to know it was costly to oppose their rule, so they made an example of their enemies, of people like Jesus.

They made an example of Jesus. In the crucifixion they showed us the way to live, the way to life. They showed us how to fight the darkness.

I gave my back to the smiters, and my cheeks to those who pulled out the beard; I hid not my face from shame and spitting. (Isa. 49:6)

On that dark Friday noon, I'm sure the forces of evil were gloating. They had killed God! They had won! They were the masters.

It didn't work out that way though.

They had misunderstood the logic of the universe. They thought that the ones on top win, when in fact the ones on the bottom are the ones who win. They thought that the strongest were the winners—the ones who killed, who inflicted the most suffering. But the ones who win are the weakest—the ones who get killed, the ones who suffer.

That's God's logic—the logic of the cross.

The last will be first, and the first last. (Matt. 20:16)

Whoever would be first among you must be slave of all. (Mark 10:44)

The one who is least among you all is the one who is great. (Luke 9:48)

Those who humble themselves like this child are the greatest in the kingdom of heaven. (Matt. 18:3; see also Matt. 19:30; 20:26–27; Mark 9:35; 10:31; Luke 13:30; 14:11; 22:26–27)

But when was the last time that the elders at your church were servants? When did they last bring the food to the church dinner? Or when did the leaders of your community last wash the dishes after a community meal?

And who cleans the toilets? (Not to mention getting crucified.)

Of course, I don't suppose Jesus literally meant that the last will be first, do you? He couldn't have meant that the church janitor was more important than the chairperson of the board of elders. And obviously that retarded kid isn't more important than the pastor.

It is not difficult to believe that when we get to heaven many of the saints will be people who were obscure, and some of today's big names will barely have made it in. But that doesn't mean that on average the best people are on the bottom rung. I mean if you have to choose between witnessing to a bum and witnessing to the president of. . . .

You don't suppose he *did* mean it, do you?

For my thoughts are not your thoughts,
    neither are your ways my ways, says the Lord.

For as the heavens are higher than the earth,
    so are my ways higher than your ways,
    and my thoughts than your thoughts. (Isa. 55:8–9)

Paul spells it out in 1 Corinthians. It's a rather complete theology of the cross—a way of life. I don't like it very much, and I don't suppose you will either.

Maybe that's why few people notice how much of the first ten chapters of 1 Corinthians (1:4–11:1) is about the cross. People think it's mostly about church fights. Which it is. But fights waged under the cross.

In the first chapter the theme of the cross is difficult to miss. Paul keeps talking about the cross: "Jews demand signs and Greeks seek wisdom, but we preach Christ crucified" (vv. 22, 23). I always thought that this phrase was about Jesus' atonement for our sins. Which it is: Jesus' suffering for us. Yet it's also a way of life, a whole new logic—not just a way of forgiveness.

Paul begins spelling out that way of life in chapter 1: for Christ sent me "to preach the gospel, and not with eloquent wisdom, lest the cross of Christ be emptied of its power" (v. 17). Apparently Paul didn't use a lot of learned arguments; he didn't mention his graduate degrees from Tarsus University and Jerusalem Seminary.

Apparently he wasn't a flashy preacher, either. Maybe he wasn't even a good one. Probably he droned on too long, or maybe he had a speech impediment. In 2 Corinthians, his critics say, "His bodily presence is weak and his speech of no account" (2 Cor. 10:10). But to God the content is what matters.

Now I always knew that. What I hadn't noticed was how well his poor speaking fits with the meaning of the cross. Unimpressive speaking is part of the way of the cross.

You see, the cross wasn't very impressive either.

He had no form or comeliness that we should look at him and no beauty that we should desire him. (Isa. 53:2)

People often point out what a varied group of people gathered around Jesus and how unhomogeneous the early church was. They point to Joanna, the wife of Herod's steward (Luke 8:3), and Manaen, a member of Herod's court (Acts 13:1). And they're right—within limits. The limits are that not many from the upper classes joined.

The chairperson of the philosophy department didn't join. And neither did the president of the Rotarians. Nor the highest paid first baseman. Nor Herod. Nor the ace reporter from the *Times.*

The vast majority of Jesus' followers were somewhere between scum and undistinguished middle class. They kind of fit in with the cross.

But the Corinthian church didn't think of themselves in that light. They thought they were part of the smart set. Some of them were eloquent and sophisticated. Soon they might be flying off to Rome to become part of the government.

Over against that, Paul put the cross.

For the word of the cross is folly to those who are perishing, but to us who are being saved it is the power of God. For it is written, "I will destroy the wisdom of the wise, and the cleverness of the clever I will thwart." Where is the wise person? Where is the scribe? Where is the debater of this age? Has not God made foolish the wisdom of the world? For Jews demand signs and Greeks seek wisdom, but we preach Christ crucified, a stumbling block to Jews and folly to Gentiles. (1 Cor. 1:18–20, 22–23)

It is through weakness that powerful evil is brought to nothing. And 1 Corinthians 2 continues the theme. "I did not come proclaiming to you the testimony of God in lofty words of wisdom. For I decided to know nothing among you except Jesus Christ and him crucified" (vv. 1, 2). No Christian Einsteins to show that Christians are as good as the world. No brilliant economic plans that finally overcome the technical problems of development.

The idea behind all those things is to impress people so much that they can't help becoming Christians. But impressing people into the kingdom is not God's plan. That is not the idea. That is not it at all. That would lead them into some other kingdom.

God's plan is Christ Jesus and him crucified. "I was with you in weakness and in much fear and trembling, and my speech and my message were not in plausible words of wisdom" (vv. 3, 4).

Which doesn't mean that Paul is opposed to wisdom. Rather he imparts "a secret and hidden wisdom" (v. 7). God's wisdom. And the world doesn't recognize it as wisdom—especially the wise and the rich. "None of the rulers of this age understood it" (v. 8). They're too busy being impressed and impressive to have any sense. So they crucified Jesus. Made an example of him.

Which is the secret wisdom: Weakness is the victor, the true power. And now through the Spirit we have that wisdom, "We have the mind of Christ" (v. 16). Astonishing thought. And it's stated in the present indicative: Not that we might have it, not that we will have it, not that we could have it, not even that we should have it. Rather, we *do* have it.

Of course, it will probably lead to some crucifixion. At least that is where Jesus' wisdom led him.

No one comprehends the thoughts of God except the Spirit of God. Unspiritual people do not receive the gifts of the Spirit of God for they are folly to them, and they are not able to understand them because they are spiritually discerned. (1 Cor. 2:11, 14)

Chapter 3 says the same thing all over again. When you come right down to it, only one thing counts and that's Jesus. "No other foundation can anyone lay than that which is laid, which is Jesus Christ" (v. 11).

We get all caught up in how smart we are. We're going to show the world how it's done. But that's not the idea. That's not it at all.

Those among you who think that you are wise in this age should become fools that you may become wise. For the wisdom of this world is folly to God. For it is written, "He catches the wise in their craftiness," and again, "The Lord knows that the thoughts of the wise are futile." (1 Cor. 3:18, 19–20)

Chapter 4 gets more specific. We aren't to be all puffed up but are to be like the apostles. And the apostles aren't kings, emperors, or rulers of any kind. They are the "last of all" (v. 9), "like men sentenced to death." (Who does that remind you of?) "A spectacle to the world." "Fools for Christ's sake." "Weak." "Held in disrepute" (vv. 9, 10).

"To the present hour we hunger and thirst, we are ill-clad and buffeted and homeless, and we labor, working with our own hands" (1 Cor. 4:11, 12). A terrible waste, don't you think? A man like Paul not having enough to eat? And if he had been properly dressed, think how many more people would have followed Jesus. And making tents for a living! Why, if he hadn't wasted time doing that, he could have written a dozen more epistles to be included in the Bible.

"When reviled, we bless; when persecuted, we endure; when slandered, we try to conciliate" (vv. 12, 13). No wonder this wisdom is scorned by the world. Next Paul will suggest turning the other cheek, or provoking people till they crucify you. There's no future in that.

"We have become, and are now, as the refuse of the world, the off-scouring of all things" (v. 13).

That's the way of the cross.

"I urge you, then, be imitators of me" (v. 16), and bear your cross.

Christ also suffered for you, leaving you an example, that you should follow in his steps. When he was reviled, he did not revile in turn; when he suffered, he did not threaten. He himself bore our sins in his body on the tree, that we might die to sin and live to righteousness. By his wounds you have been healed. (1 Peter 2:21, 23, 24)

Chapter 6 gets even more specific about the way of the cross. If you Christians have disputes with each other, Paul says, don't go to court. Settle it within the church. And if that fails, let yourself be cheated.

It's a ridiculous idea, of course. It wouldn't work. It's almost as silly as the Sermon on the Mount. Paul can't mean what he says literally (though any figurative meaning isn't obvious).

Churches have been known to leave denominations because

the denominations denied inerrancy. And then get involved in lawsuits over whether the property belonged to the local church or to the denomination. It's a matter of principle, of course.

There's more than one way to deny inerrancy.

> He was oppressed, and he was afflicted,
>   yet he opened not his mouth;
> like a lamb that is led to the slaughter,
>   and like a sheep that before its shearers is dumb,
> so he opened not his mouth. (Isa. 53:7)

Chapter 7 deals with marriage, marriage under the cross. That kind of marriage means not putting your own interests and desires first. The other person is first. When it comes to sex in marriage, you don't control your own body: You do what the other person wants. That's not exactly what they advise in assertiveness training, but it sounds like the way of the cross: "For the wife does not rule over her own body, but the husband does; likewise the husband does not rule over his body, but the wife does" (v. 4). Can you imagine what marriage would be like if both partners were dedicated to serving the other?

And when it comes to divorce when one spouse is not a Christian, the Christian should stay in the marriage as long as the other wants. Which wouldn't always be easy (vv. 12–16).

If you're single, marriage might be more pleasurable but don't do it if you can help yourself. It will cause distraction. Marriage makes it harder to go wherever you're needed in the kingdom, harder to do whatever needs to be done. You'll be torn between the kingdom and your family (7:25–38).

(I told you you wouldn't like the ethics of the cross. Maybe the wisdom of the world is preferable.)

If you come to me and do not hate your own father and mother and wife and children and brothers and sisters, yes, and even your own life, you cannot be my disciple. If you do not bear your own cross and come after me, you cannot be my disciple. (Luke 14:26–27)

In chapter 8, Paul discusses eating food given to idols. Some of the Corinthians held that it was all right to eat food offered to idols because they knew that idols were not really gods. And they were right, technically, but not everyone in the church understood. Some of them, if they ate temple food, might get sucked back into the temple worship. So Paul says, "If food is a cause of my brother or sister falling, I will never eat meat" (8:13).

A pattern is emerging. The way of the cross is becoming all too clear. It's not always spectacular like a public nailing to a cross. Usually, it's just tiring. Maybe I could handle the spectacular parts (and then again, maybe not), but the dailiness of the cross is hard—like Chinese water torture. Drip. Drip. Drip.

If you would come after me, deny yourself and take up your cross daily. (Luke 9:23)

The way of the cross, the suffering, the endurance, the forgetting about ourselves, the serving of others, the crucifixion, the daily self-sacrifice—they are what quench evil.

What that means for us is all too clear. And too clearly contrary to our hedonistic culture. The wisdom of God is not very popular, which isn't very surprising if you're dealing with the fashion industry, or even with secular psychologists.

But the church? And Christian political activists? Have they bought the wisdom of the world too? Thereby letting the world go to hell?

Let there be no mistake. Our models should not be successful people like Grace Kelly, Jack Kennedy, Albert Einstein, or John D. Rockefeller—not even C. S. Lewis. Our model is Jesus Christ.

> He was despised and rejected;
>   a man of sorrows acquainted with grief;
> and as one from whom people hide their faces,
>   he was despised, and we esteemed him not. (Isa. 53:3)

21. God

But I haven't told the whole story. It is not just our suffering, serving, and weakness that dampen the fires of evil. It is God. And it didn't all start with Jesus. The weak won in the Old Testament, too. Or rather God acted on their behalf there, too. You could almost say that's what the Old Testament is about—trusting God rather than your own strength.

But I'm getting ahead of myself again.

You may have noticed that some of what I quoted from 1 Corinthians was cut off in mid-sentence. For example, I quoted, "God chose what is poor and despised in the world, even things that are not, to bring to nothing things that are" (1:28), and I stopped there. But Paul continues, "so that no human being might boast in the presence of God" (1:29).

I was stressing the low and despised, which is quite right. But Paul was also stressing God. Paul was telling the Corinthians that they weren't such hot stuff. But that would probably only have increased the turmoil in Corinth. He went on to say that God is the only one who is hot stuff. They weren't so wise, but even if they were, that kind of wisdom amounts to nothing compared to God.

By and large, God doesn't choose to use graduates of Harvard School of Business, Rhodes scholars, or self-made millionaires. By and large, God uses nobodies. That's what I've been saying, and it's what Paul says.

But I've been emphasizing the nobodies whereas Paul emphasizes God just as much. Paul does not mean that the weak and despised have a natural moral power that the strong and respected don't have. He means that God's might is so great that even by using nobodies God gets things done. God chooses to act that way so people won't think they did anything themselves. That way people will see that God is the one who acts.

In an odd section at the end of 2 Corinthians (chapters 10–13), Paul says something similar. Here Paul defends his authority as an apostle and can't avoid boasting. But he boasts of his suffering and weakness—they are the evidence of his apostleship: "If I must boast, I will boast of the things that show my weakness" (11:30). He boasts of his sufferings: poverty, beatings, stoning, shipwrecks, imprisonments (11:7–15, 23–33).

Then he boasts of a "thorn in the flesh" (12:7), probably a physical problem. Three times he asked God to take it away, but God refused. God wanted him to be weak, not for the sake of weakness as such, but so he could have God's power. God told him, "My power is made perfect in weakness" (12:9). Then Paul continues: "I will all the more gladly boast of my weakness, that the power of Christ may rest on me. For the sake of Christ, then, I am content with weakness, insults, hardships, persecutions, and calamities; for when I am weak, then I am strong" (12:9, 10).

God chooses to use the weak. Something about weakness lets God's strength through. Our weakness is an entryway for God.

This theme is clear in the life of Christ. It appears in his place of birth, the unimportance of his family, his choice of disciples, the people he helped—in practically everything—and especially his death. God's mightiest intervention in human history was through the weakness of the crucifixion.

But is the theme of weakness found in the Old Testament? It is, but it's not always obvious. Genesis, for example, does not exactly stress the point. It does not even mention the weakness of Adam, Eve, Abel, Enoch, Methusaleh, or Noah—at least not as an entryway for God. And it makes a point of the power and wealth of Abraham, Isaac, Jacob, and Joseph.

Nonetheless, even in Genesis weakness emerges as a theme. Consider Isaac's birth. Abraham and Sarah were old—too old to have a child. God promised them a son, but they were not fools. They knew they couldn't have children. Even when she was young, Sarah had been barren, and now she had entered menopause. And Abraham was a hundred years old. God's promise was so silly Sarah laughed. Wouldn't you?

So Abraham and Sarah got busy and figured out what needed to be done. Relying on their own strength, they arranged for Abraham to have a child by a slave (Gen. 15:1–6, 16:1–6). They were practical.

But that was not God's plan. It was too sensible, too practical. It left God out. God wanted to use weak old Sarah, not a young, fertile woman (Gen. 17:15–21; 18:9–16; 21:1–7). Sarah's weakness was an entryway for God.

And then there's Abraham's call to sacrifice Isaac (Gen. 22). I do not understand that story very well, but one thing stands out. Sacrificing Isaac was not practical. In fact, it didn't make sense. For Abraham to sacrifice Isaac was to weaken himself. That is the way of God, even in Genesis.

But what about the wealth and power of Abraham, Isaac, and Jacob? Doesn't that weigh against the idea of God's using weakness? Maybe, but there are some other factors. Notice the oddness of Abraham's route to greatness. He and his family left their home and their kindred to become wandering migrants. They left their security to enter the unknown—at God's command. They acted rather like some fishermen who left their nets to follow Jesus. It was silly and impractical. They entered into weakness.

As for Jacob, he was not the kind of man I'd choose as an example. He was a rascal, a schemer, cheating everyone in sight. But God chose him anyway. God's choice was what counted, not Jacob's power or righteousness.

Besides, Abraham, Isaac, and Jacob were not as mighty as we sometimes think. They were certainly wealthy people, but they weren't in the league, say, of the pharaohs. At most, they were leaders of a minor nomadic tribe. If Pharaoh had been told that they were the children of God, he would have laughed harder than Sarah.

My arguing that Abraham, Isaac, and Jacob were weak may sound like special pleading (I worry about it myself), but the rest of the Bible sees the patriarchs that way. Psalm 105 is a short history of the children of Israel. The Israelites recited it at festivals to remind themselves of their roots. What it reminded them of was not the wealth of Abraham, Isaac, and Jacob. Rather, it reminded them that "they were few in number, of little account, and sojourners, wandering from nation to nation" (Ps. 105:12, 13; see also Isa. 51:2). It stressed that they were nobodies. And, reminiscent of 1 Corinthians, it combined this stress with a stress on the greatness of God. In their weakness "God allowed no one to oppress them and rebuked kings on their account" (105:14). Their weakness was an entryway for God's greatness.

Hebrews 11 makes the same point. "By faith Abraham obeyed when he was called to go out, and he went out, not knowing where he was to go. By faith he sojourned in a land of promise, as in a foreign land" (Heb. 11:8–9). Abraham's action was foolish weakness.

Deuteronomy 26:5 portrays Jacob in this same way. That verse is probably the start of an ancient creedal statement comparable to the Apostle's Creed for Christians. It begins, "A wandering Aramean was my father, and he went down to Egypt and sojourned there, few in number."

Then there is Joseph. He was one of the most powerful people in the world—second only to the pharaoh. He could hardly be considered merely the head of a minor nomadic tribe. But God used him anyway. He is the prototype of God's using the great.

And that's no problem. Paul says that not many were wise, not many were noble. He doesn't say that *none* were wise or noble. And Jesus says it's *hard* for the rich to enter the kingdom. He doesn't say it's *impossible.*

So maybe Joseph is the exception.

But I'm saying that with a few exceptions God chooses to

use the weak and poor. I've started with Abraham, Isaac, Jacob, and Joseph—all of whom are exceptions to the rule to one degree or another. Sarah is the only one to fit the rule comfortably. (Soon we will examine the case of Moses, the biggest exception of them all.)

It's one thing to admit exceptions; it's another to claim that most people are exceptions.

But the case is not as bad as it sounds. I am not saying that God doesn't give the weak power. I am not saying God wouldn't empower a poor person to become, for example, president of the United States. I am saying rather that the one God chooses will be surprising—someone weak and foolish. God chooses failures to become president, not people who connive for power. Not those who go to the best schools so they can serve the poor more effectively. God gives power to losers.

Joseph is a perfect example, and Abraham and Jacob aren't far behind. They were losers whom *God* lifted up. That's the point.

Joseph was the biggest loser around. His brothers hated him and sold him as a slave—not too propitious a start. As a slave he was imprisoned on a sex charge! How much lower and weaker can you get?

Then God raised him up and gave him great power.

That suggests a whole different mind-set than you usually find among Christian political activists. We are dedicated to a strategy of effectiveness that leaves God out. We're busy backing the best available Democrat who has a reasonable chance of winning. Meanwhile God backs losers. God's candidate would be an illegal Hispanic immigrant rotting in prison on a trumped-up sex charge. How would you like someone like that for president? The whole idea is absurd, of course, but then so is God. (Not, however, as absurd as forty thousand kids dying each day while pragmatists run the world.)

If God decides to act, I'll bet Christian political activists will have their backs turned. They'll think God's candidate is silly, and they'll back someone more effective.

And then there's Moses. He didn't start off very well, of course. The child of a slave, he was condemned to death as a baby. He soon had all the privileges: childhood in the palace, connections with the royal family, the best training, and probably a position of responsibility.

Then at forty he had a midlife crisis. And he blew it in a big way. He couldn't wait for God, and he took things into his own hands. He got busy and prepared to lead the revolution. He appointed himself defender of justice and executioner of oppressors.

But that was not God's way, or at least not God's time. So Moses became a fugitive. On the backside of the desert. Herding sheep. It's dumber than Jesus being a carpenter or Paul a tentmaker. He wasted the whole middle of his life, his most productive years, when he could have been most effective.

But God wasn't concerned about Moses' effectiveness. Of course, when the time came, Moses wasn't so sure he wanted to take charge of Israel. He thought that he was nobody, that someone else should do it. "Who am I that I should" do this great thing? (Exod. 3:11). The Israelites won't believe me (4:1). "I am not eloquent" enough; I don't speak well (4:10). (Remember Paul's comments on his own speaking?)

God's answer was simple: God agreed. Moses couldn't do it, but God could. "I will be with you" (3:12). "Who has made the human mouth? Is it not I, the Lord?" (4:11). God was angered by Moses' excuses, but at least Moses was no longer angling for the job. He was no longer a scheming, self-appointed, revolutionary leader. I suspect that's why God had left Moses in the wilderness: God wanted him to come to the end of himself. Then Moses was ready for God to put him to use. Not when he completed his training at Cairo University, but when he no longer believed he could do it. When he *was* a loser and knew it.

And the children of Israel! They were not exactly winners themselves. They were a bunch of slaves, disobeying God at every possible turn and griping. They must have set a world record for griping. That was the motley crew God chose.

At least the Hebrew slaves didn't believe they could free themselves or even take care of themselves once they were free. But the trouble was they didn't believe God could do it either. And the history of their wanderings in the wilderness is the history of their learning to believe, of their learning to trust God to do impossible things through their weakness.

The Exodus was not due to Moses' brilliant leadership or the Israelites' courageous resistance. The Exodus was the result of God's action. Moses and the Israelites were little more than reluctant bystanders. The foundation of the Exodus was God's statement: "I have seen the affliction of my people, and I have come down to deliver them" (Exod. 3:7, 8). God may have used Moses, but it was God who freed Israel.

In Greek mythology, Moses would have been a god, or at least a demigod, whose mighty deeds freed Israel. In a fairy tale, he would have been a great sorcerer who could produce plagues. In Marxist thought, he would have been a brilliant soldier who led guerrilla armies. In populist theory, he would have been a community organizer who helped people see their oppression. In secular pacifism, he would have been a genius at nonviolent direct action whose moral force brought the Egyptian empire to its knees.

But in the Bible *God* produced the plagues, using humble, broken Moses to announce them. Which is quite different. That is Christian politics, and when we think about politics in any other way, we are not thinking biblical politics.

The story of Israel's journey to Canaan makes the same point, again and again. As soon as the Israelites left Egypt, Pharaoh had them followed. They despaired, of course, but Moses told them: "See the salvation which the Lord will work for you today. The Lord will fight for you, and you have only to be still" (Exod. 14:13, 14).

Then God opened the Red Sea while the Israelites crossed—

and closed it while the Egyptians were crossing. For us it tends to be pious words to say, "The Lord is my strength and my song. The Lord has become my salvation" (Exod. 15:2). But on that day those words of Miriam were real to Israel; they meant the words literally. *The Lord* was their strength and salvation.

The rest of the journey is more of the same. Israel twice despairs over lack of food, and God provides it (Exod. 16 and Num. 11). Twice they complain about lack of water, and God provides it (Exod. 17:1–7; Num. 20:2–13). The Amalekites attack, and Israel beats them—not because they are strong but because God fights for them when Moses has his arms raised (Exod. 17:8–16). God's help is less spectacular but just as real when they defeat the Canaanites (Num. 21:1–3), the Amorites (Num. 21:21–30), Og, king of Bashan (Num. 21:31–35), and the Midianites (Num. 31:1–12).

The point is made in more detail the first time Israel arrives at Canaan. Their spies tell them that the people who dwell there are giants with large, well-fortified cities that Israel is too weak to conquer (13:28–29, 31–33). Caleb and Joshua do not disagree about the facts or tell the Israelites that they are strong enough to conquer Canaan. They say instead, "If the Lord delights in us, the Lord will bring us into this land and give it to us" (14:8, 9).

Victory and defeat have nothing to do with the people's strength but only with God's intervention.[1] That conviction is at the heart of any action that is genuinely Christian. It must be the center of Christian political action.

The rest of the history of Israel continues the same theme. The story of Jericho is a stunning example. To start with, the only inhabitant who helped the Israelites was a nobody. Rahab was the kind of person Jesus went around with—a prostitute who became a hero of the faith (Heb. 11:31).

Then God divided the Jordan for Israel to cross—not something Joshua could have done too well by himself. God did this "so that all the peoples of the earth may know that the hand of the Lord is mighty" (Josh. 4:24). Then God gave Joshua instructions. March around Jericho blowing trumpets (Josh. 6).

I can just imagine Joshua's face: "Sure, Lord, we can bring yo-yo's, too, if you want, but what shall we use for battering rams? How about that new MX model I read about in *Time* magazine? I hear it's pretty effective." But that was not God's way. Strength and effectiveness are never God's plan.

That is the theme of the book of Joshua. I am not fond of the slaughter reported there, but oddly enough Joshua contains the essential kernel of pacifism: trusting God in our weakness. Israel's defeats at Ai, the sun standing still at Gibeon, and all the rest of the bloody record make one point—what happens is up to God (Josh. 2:10–11; 6:16; 10:11–14; 11:4–8; 23:3, 9–10; 24:12).

Judges continues the tradition. The message is that when Israel disobeys God, God intervenes to punish them. When they seek God, God miraculously frees them. Their freedom has nothing to do with their strength, only with their spirituality.

The most striking example is Gideon. God tells Gideon to deliver Israel from Midian, and he replies: "I ask you, Lord, how can I deliver Israel? Behold, my clan is the weakest in Manasseh, and I am the least in my family" (Judges 6:15). Here we have another revolutionary leader like Moses who didn't want the job or think he could do it. Again, God did not assure Gideon he could do it. When Gideon proclaims his weakness, God more or less agrees, replying simply, "But I will be with you" (6:16).

When the Midianites and their allies came, they were "like locusts for multitude, and their camels were without number." Gideon raised a small but substantial army (thirty-two thousand), but God wanted a smaller army "that Israel may not boast against me that their own strength has saved them" (7:2). So we have the insanity of three hundred men choosing weakness and attacking the Midianite host—by blowing trumpets, breaking jars, and flashing torches.

The rest of the historical books of the Old Testament keep pounding away at the same thing. Our strength has nothing to do with anything. God is all that counts. To make that point, God uses our weakness.

1 Samuel opens with Hannah's despair over her weakness: she has no children, and her husband's other wife taunts her about it. So God gives Samuel to Hannah, and she sings a song (the model for Mary's song in Luke 1).

> The bows of the mighty are broken,
>   but the feeble gird on strength.
> Those who were full have hired themselves out for bread,
>   but those who were hungry have ceased to hunger.
> The barren has borne seven,
>   but she who has many children is forlorn.
> It is not by strength that a person prevails. (1 Sam. 2:4–5, 9)

Samuel was a small boy, not of the priestly line nor even a Levite. But God used him. God spoke to him not to the high priest, or to the high priest's family (1 Sam. 3).

And don't forget Saul. True, he was tall, strong, and handsome. But when God chose him to be king, he replied, "Am I not a Benjaminite, from the least of the tribes of Israel? And is not my family the humblest of all the families of the tribe of Benjamin? Why then have you spoken to me in this way?" (1 Sam. 9:21). And when it came time to crown Saul king, he was so reluctant that he went and hid (10:20–24).

Then there's David. A mere shepherd. He was so unimpressive that his own father didn't call him to meet Samuel. His oldest brother was handsome and strong, and Samuel was ready to anoint him king. But God told Samuel: "Do not look on his appearance or his height; for the Lord sees not as you see. You look on outward appearances, but the Lord looks on the heart" (16:7). God, typically, chose the youngest (who, however, was also handsome and had beautiful eyes).

And his meeting with Goliath! It's in the league of the story of Gideon or the fall of Jericho. It has become a paradigm of weakness defeating strength. When David hears how Goliath is defying Israel, he doesn't claim he is strong enough to defeat him. He says, "Who is this uncircumcised Philistine that he should defy the armies of the living God?" (17:26). Saul tries to dissuade David from fighting: "You are but a youth" (17:33). Then he offers David armor, but when David puts it on, he can hardly waddle. So he goes out with only his staff, five smooth stones, and a sling.

When Goliath first spots David, he says, "Am I a dog that you come to me with sticks? Come to me, and I will give your flesh to the birds of air and to the beasts of the fields" (17:43, 44). David replies, "You come to me with a sword and with a spear and with a javelin, but I come to you in the name of the Lord of hosts. This day the Lord will deliver you into my hand, and I will strike you down that all the earth may know that there is a God in Israel who saves not with sword and spear; for the battle is the Lord's" (17:45, 46, 47). Then David kills Goliath.

God used David's weakness.

That God's strength is what counts is a point made often in David's story (2 Sam. 5:10; 7:8–10; 22:28–30; 23:10, 12). It is made even when David's military might is recognized. But another story about David requires attention. The Bible has two stories about David's sins. One is well known: his adultery with Bathsheba and his murder of her husband. The other is not so well known, perhaps because it's less titillating, or perhaps because our culture doesn't recognize it as sin. What David did was to count the number of men who were able to fight (2 Sam. 24). In other words, he took a census.

So what's the big deal here? The big deal is that David delights in it (24:3). He is pleased at how strong his army is, so David isn't trusting God.

That's one of the pitfalls of having a king. It is hard for a king to trust God. At first he may be an insignificant person whom God raises up. But soon he grows strong, and his sons are princes and so are even less likely than their father to think of themselves as nobodies. The Old Testament records the rise of the monarchy, but it records it with considerable unease.

The opening of the book of Kings puts less emphasis on weakness than some books, but even there, Israel is evaluated by its spiritual state, not by its military preparedness. It rises and falls according to its relationship to God, not according to how many chariots and horses it has.

Solomon is vastly wealthy and powerful, and this fortune is considered to be due to his righteousness. But even Kings returns to the theme of weakness. Wicked old King Ahab is attacked. The Syrian king, Benhadad, comes with a multitude, and Ahab can only muster seven thousand soldiers. Benhadad contemptuously orders them taken alive, but God wants Ahab to see who is the Lord, so God defeats Benhadad. The next year Benhadad attacks again, and the people of Israel are "like two little flocks of goats, but the Syrians filled the country" (20:27). And God defeats the Syrians.

2 Kings (really the same book as 1 Kings) is full of the theme of God's intervention on the side of the weak (2 Kings 1:12; 3:4–27; 5:11; 8:13; 13:4, 5, 14; 14:27). Early on, the Syrians attack again and hold the Israelites under siege so that the people are forced to eat their own children (6:24–31). Israel's weakness is complete. At that point God decides to deliver them, using no army at all. Rather the Syrians imagine they hear an attacking army and flee (7:6–7). And it is not the king or the nobility who discover their flight but four starving lepers.[2] How much weaker can you get?

Most of the Prophets clearly proclaim the same message. If the first great event in Israel's history is the Exodus, the second is the exile. The great powers are at war: Assyria, Egypt, and Babylon are all out to conquer each other, the world, and everything in between. Israel and Judah are in between.

Things do not look good. The job of the prophets is to explain what is going on and what the children of Israel should do. One striking thing is that the prophets do not address Israel's predicament as an accident of history. They do not say: "Sorry, you got caught in the middle." (Which is what any historian would say.) Nor do they address it as a technological failure or a lack of military preparedness: "You should have spent more of the GNP on chariots and had your scientists design a spear that Nebuchadnezzar wasn't ready for."

No, they address the predicament as a moral and spiritual problem. God is great enough to stop Babylonia and Assyria cold in their tracks anytime the children of Israel change their ways. All they have to do is abandon injustice, idolatry, adultery, oppression, and Sabbath breaking.

It is not military strength that is at issue. It is spiritual strength.

It is striking how often the prophets return to the theme of relying on God rather than on military strength or human might. They denounce oppression, adultery, and injustice in living color, but the heart of their message is that the children of Israel must trust God and stop rebelling.

Given the military situation, kings naturally wanted to get one of the superpowers to protect them from the others. But the prophets didn't like that. They wanted the kings to get their protection from God. So when Judah makes a pact with Egypt against Assyria, Isaiah's words are harsh:

> Woe to those who go down to Egypt for help
>   and rely on horses,
> who trust in chariots because they are many
>   and in horsemen because they are very strong,
> but do not look to the holy one of Israel.
> The Egyptians are human and not God;
>   and their horses are flesh and not spirit.
> When the Lord stretches out a hand,
>   the helper will stumble and the one helped will fall,
>   and they will all perish together. (Isa. 31:1, 3)

But Isaiah has a solution, a solution as impractical and bizarre then as it would be now:

> In returning and rest you shall be saved;
> in quietness and in trust shall be your strength. (Isa. 30:15)

No longer was Judah to send emissaries to every kingdom they could think of in a desperate effort to get allies, horses, and chariots. They were to relax and leave it to God. Silly, wasn't it?[3]

God is the one in charge. Kings, kingdoms, and armies rise and fall at God's merest whim; it has nothing to do with their own strength or wisdom. A story in Daniel makes the point with color.

One night Nebuchadnezzar was resting in his palace when he was frightened by a dream. The dream teaches that "the Most High rules over people and their kingdoms and sets up kings at will from the lowliest of people" (Dan. 4:17). Daniel tells him that the dream means he is going to lose his mind and live like an animal for one year.

> At the end of twelve months [Nebuchadnezzar] was walking on the roof of the royal palace of Babylon, and the king said, "Is not this great Babylon, which I have built by my mighty power as a royal residence and for the glory of my majesty?" While the words were still in the king's mouth, there fell a voice from heaven, "O King Nebuchadnezzar, to you it is spoken: The kingdom has departed from you, and you shall be driven from among people, and your dwelling shall be with the beasts of the field until you have learned that the Most High rules over people and their kingdoms." (Dan. 4:29–31, 32)

Isaiah 40 says the same thing, but in a very different tone. One of the most beautiful chapters in the Bible starts with a call to comfort God's people (vv. 1–2), for God is coming to set things right (vv. 3–5). God will feed the people like a shepherd feeds his flock and will hold them tenderly like a shepherd holds lambs (vv. 9–11). This shepherd is the God who measures the oceans in the hollow of one hand, before whom nations (led by men like Nebuchadnezzar and Sargon) are like the dust on scales (vv. 12–26):

God brings princes to nought
  and makes the rulers of the earth as nothing.
God gives power to the faint
  and increases the strength of the one who has no might.
Even youths shall faint and be weary,
  and the young shall fall exhausted;
but they who wait for the Lord shall renew their strength,
  they shall mount up with wings like eagles,
they shall run and not be weary,
  they shall walk and not faint. (vv. 23, 29–31)

God brings the strong to nothing but strengthens the weak—if they wait patiently, not relying on their own abilities.

The message of the prophets, of the whole Old Testament, is summarized by a sentence from Zechariah, "Not by might, nor by power, but by my Spirit, says the Lord of hosts" (Zech. 4:6).

God uses weakness to put out the fires of evil.

22. The Cross or the Slingshot?

God may use weakness to put out the fires of evil, but personally I prefer violence. The model God gave as the way to deal with evil was a suffering servant. On a cross.

But our way, the way we choose naturally, is not quite the same. We prefer the bomb. Which comes from a different spirit.

Not that I'm a pacifist. Not completely anyway. I've been prevented from becoming a doctrinaire pacifist by God's apparent approval of violence in the Old Testament—and in a few places in the New Testament, for that matter.[1]

What's more, my heart is not always in nonviolence. I suspect I'd have joined Bonhoeffer in trying to assassinate Hitler (if I'd had the guts). And I have a deep sympathy for Ernesto Cardenal's leaving Solentiname to join the guerrillas fighting Somoza.

I mean, the guerrillas who fought Somoza seem to me to have been a modern version of David and Goliath. (Many of them were even Christians.) And isn't Nicaragua's resisting Reagan and the U.S. war machine like Hezekiah's resisting Sennacherib and the Assyrian war machine? In fact, the whole history of Nicaragua could be right out of the Old Testament. All we need now is for God to send a flood just when a large body of Contras try to cross the Coco River into Nicaragua.

And yet . . . and yet . . . what about the cross?

The cross is the model of love and weakness, of turning the other cheek and suffering for others. The bomb is the model of destruction and retaliation, of strength and making others suffer. Christians cannot follow the spirit of the bomb. We are under the cross.

But what of the Old Testament? Surely the Old Testament

supports the spirit of the bomb? No, even the Old Testament rejects the spirit of the bomb.

Take the story of David and Goliath. What some people notice about it is the killing. David killed Goliath. The story is scarcely nonviolent (which is why I'm not quite a pacifist).

But David did it with a slingshot. A slingshot and God. That's what other people notice. And that's a rejection of the bomb. The army of Israel was waiting for a mighty warrior to champion them against Goliath. (They wanted a bomb.) What they got was a kid who had never been in battle before. Saul wanted him at least to wear armor. But David's only armor was God. He went in weakness.

In fact, the story of David and Goliath is a decisive rejection of militarism, of the whole idea of peace through strength. Peace is not the result of military might greater than the enemy's. Peace does not grow out of horses, tanks, or missiles; it does not grow out of alliances with the powerful. Peace is the gift of God, and it grows out of relying on God rather than the bomb; it grows out of righteousness and justice. That is the message of half the stories in the Old Testament, and it is the message of the poets and the prophets. But I will quote only two passages here:

A king is not saved by his great army;
    a warrior is not delivered by his great strength.
The war horse is a vain hope for victory,
    and by its great might it cannot save.
Behold the eye of the Lord is on those who fear God. (Ps. 33:16-17,
    18, 19)

Put not your trust in princes,
    in a human being, in whom there is no help.
Happy is the one whose help is the God of Jacob. (Ps. 146:3, 5)

So the Old Testament rejects militarism out of hand. How teachings to ancient Israel should apply to the United States today is not terribly clear, but this much is crystal clear: The Old Testament gives not one ounce of support to the idea of peace through strength. Those who cite the Old Testament to defend the bomb and the mighty U.S. war machine have not read carefully. In the Old Testament, the weak are the ones who experience shalom.

Goliaths are slain.

But that argument against militarism is scarcely an argument for pacifism. Goliath was slain. David killed him.

Perhaps it is time for a David to rise up in countries like Nicaragua. Maybe a new version of Bonhoeffer's assassination plot would be in order. Maybe we Christians should go to Nicaragua, taking our .22 rifles with us, and there fight Goliath. The odds against us would be nearly as great as those against David. What chance do .22s have against machine guns and helicopters? But perhaps God would once again intervene and kill Goliath.

Yet, what about the cross? In the shadow of the cross, can we kill even in those circumstances? I think not. If we Christians were to take the cross as our model, we would still go to Nicaragua to fight Goliath, only this time we'd go without weapons (except for God). We'd go where Contras are likely to attack (like oil depots and border towns) and put our bodies between the Contras and their targets. Our only protection would be God. And American Christians unable to go to Nicaragua would at least haunt Congress, attend demonstrations, and refuse to pay taxes.

Who then should we follow? David or Jesus? Notice, those are our only options. We do not have the option of joining the marines to go kill more Central Americans. Militarism and militarily enforced oppression are wrong. Nor do we have the option of silence, of neutrality, of business as usual. That route is simply a different form of violence against the oppressed. It is hidden, but it is just as violent as a gun.

So what is to be our model? Not the bomb. Not silence. Is it to be the cross or the slingshot? Should we follow Jesus or David?

Just putting the question that way answers it. Of course we should follow Jesus. Christ's coming to earth, and especially the crucifixion and resurrection, are the crucial events of human history. David and Goliath simply are not in the same league as God crucified.

And if you put at least some stock in the idea of progressive revelation, you can see that David's view of violence when he challenged Goliath is a big step forward compared to Goliath's view, or Saul's. It is a rejection of the militarism of their (and our) day. In fact, it is at least halfway to the spirit of nonviolence expressed in the cross. And the New Testament goes the rest of the way.

Christians are not under the slingshot. We are under the cross.

But perhaps the cross was only for forgiveness. Perhaps it was not intended to show us how to live, how to deal with violence. And what about the sword the state has in Romans 13:4? Perhaps turning the other cheek (Rom. 12:14-21) is only for individuals and not for nations.

I find this terribly complicated. A good lawyer could argue this to four different conclusions—all compelling. Can the state use violence that individuals shouldn't? Certainly government officials have authority which private individuals don't. (The police are in fact different from vigilantes.) But someone killed by a policeman's bullet is just as dead as someone killed by the Mafia. A child burned by napalm is in just as much pain as one burned by a private arsonist.

So do we follow the Old Testament or the Sermon on the Mount? Romans 13 or Romans 12? Just war theory or the cross? I can appreciate most of the argument for both sides. So I have never quite persuaded myself of pacifism.

However, I suspect that all these arguments miss the point and distract us from the real issue. And the real issue is the spirit in which we live. Do we live in the spirit of the cross or the spirit of retaliation? I realize how simplistic that is, but perhaps it is time we became as simple as children. Children can understand that killing is killing whether it's done by the Mafia or the marines. It takes a law degree to understand the difference; so perhaps it's time to give up our law degrees and our sophistication.

Granted, government officials have authority which others don't have, but I cannot believe that their authority puts them above the cross. Surely even officials are under its authority. They aren't to follow any spirit except that of the cross.

Why wouldn't the spirit which leads individuals be the one that leads nations? Why would government ethics be different from personal ethics? If a spirit is good, then it's good. If killing and stealing are bad, then they are bad—for nations as well as individuals.

The path of life (ethics, if you like) is rooted in reality. Things aren't right or wrong by the whim of God. They are wrong if they bring misery and destruction; they are right if they bring joy and shalom. The spirit of retaliation is destruction. The spirit of the cross is shalom. Turning the other cheek produces joy; hitting back produces misery. That's true for individuals *and* nations.

Modern Israel's insistence on an eye for an eye and a tooth for a tooth is a good example. It is leaving both Israel and its neighbors eyeless and toothless. And America's refusal to turn the other cheek to the Soviets (and vice versa) is producing unending escalation; it almost has to end in the antithesis of the cross—the bomb.

Let me put it another way. People often argue that the Sermon on the Mount applies only to individuals, not to governments. But my own observation is that as a rule such people don't believe it applies to them personally either. They have every intention of retaliating if someone wrongs them. Their careful arguments about nations and individuals suddenly seem to be mere words. They have missed the point. This is harsh, but I fear that most of us have no more intention of letting the spirit of the cross rule in our personal lives than our leaders do in government.

Besides, if you say certain principles apply only to individuals and not to nations, where do you draw the line? If nations need not turn the other cheek, maybe they can also lie, steal, and oppress the poor. After all, the Ten Commandments were given to individuals as surely as was the Sermon on the Mount. (And nations ignore the Ten Commandments as freely as they do the Sermon on the Mount.)

We must get beyond the detailed arguments and search for the spirit behind Scripture. The whole logic of Scripture points toward weakness, toward becoming as helpless as the poor, toward serving, toward accepting suffering for others. In other words, it points to nonviolence.

I don't mean that I have a ready explanation for those verses that seem to suggest something else. I don't. What I mean is that the overwhelming thrust of Scripture is to meet evil and violence in weakness, nonviolently. That's the logic (the spirit) behind Scripture.

When I speak in churches I often speak on poverty. What I say is that the way Christians should deal with poverty is not to become rich and use their leverage for the poor, it is to become poor like Jesus and use their weakness for the poor. When I say that, someone in the audience almost always attacks me for being a pacifist. At first I couldn't grasp why they thought I was a pacifist. But lately I have begun to see their point. They were seeing the logic of my position. And it is the logic of the Scripture. If weakness is the way to deal with poverty, it is the way to deal with violence. If Christ's death is the paradigm for dealing with evil, then violence is part of a very different paradigm.

Which raises questions about some versions of pacifism. Some pacifists forbid all killing but allow the use of force if it's not lethal. They use all their strength and sophistication to fight evil. That conforms to the rule, "Thou shalt not kill," but it seems to me to miss completely the logic of Scripture, the spirit of the cross.

Leviathan's tentacles reach throughout the world bringing misery and destruction, and the reason is that both nations and individuals serve a spirit that does not recognize the cross. We serve the spirit of the bomb.

It's killing us. And our world.

Peace can only come when we accept the spirit of the cross and begin confronting evil with weakness.

6. SERVANT LIVING

23. How Then Should We Live?

What does all this mean for our day-to-day lives? We live in a world where every moment could be a delight, but we have made a terrible mess. We have built social and economic structures that let forty thousand kids die every day because they're poor. Meanwhile a third of the marriages in America collapse, wives are battered by their husbands, and children are molested by their fathers. It's as if we've been dropped into a cage of mad dogs that are tearing us to pieces.

And what do we do about it? Maybe we take drugs to ease the pain—tobacco, heroin, alcohol, barbiturates. (Or is it so we'll die more quickly?) That response is understandable, but it doesn't help a whole lot. Alternatively, we distract ourselves with sports, fashion, learning, or status. Can you imagine someone in a cage of mad dogs drinking whiskey and watching football on television?

So the dogs are spreading our guts—spiritual and physical—all over the cage. Everyone else's guts too. And we are not fighting off the dogs. All we are fighting off is the knowledge that the dogs are there. So we complain because the newspapers don't print enough good news.

We have gone quite mad. We have lost touch with reality. We have persuaded ourselves, for example, that money is worth living for—or at least worth working for. We are selling ice boxes on the burning deck, while the dogs tear out our guts.

And we are ignoring Jesus. Some of us claim to believe *in* him, but few of us seem to believe him. Which makes believing in him kind of pointless. We'd rather earn a good living, and be devoured. And devour—the Soviets, the poor, our competitors, our families, ourselves. For we ourselves are the mad dogs.

Jesus is trying to put us back in touch with reality. Money, status, getting even are a mirage. Reality is loving and serving others. That's the way to life. That's the way to change the world.

We can have springs of living water welling up inside . . . and be human. Or we can fight for money and importance and our rights . . . like mad dogs. And continue the ruin of the world.

Once I gave a talk on the unimportance of money in solving social problems. A young social activist became irate. (Which is not unusual when I speak.) "Yes, but how do you *solve* social problems?" he asked. I concluded he wanted a simple technique for ending world hunger. So I told him it wasn't so easy; there was no button to push that would put everything right. Whereupon a young woman said, "Yes, there is. Loving and serving."

She was right, but we can't believe it. We want a technological answer or an answer about giving money to charitable organizations. When what Jesus asks is lives of love and service.

But what would a way of life be that centered on loving and serving? How do you follow Jesus in the humdrum of daily life—when the dramatic things that happen are mostly on television? How should the peace activist live at home? What does it mean to follow Jesus . . . after you've sold your possessions and given to the poor? Those are vital questions, but questions that are not very seriously wrestled with. I guess it's easier to criticize the Soviets or carry signs in demonstrations than to seriously consider the day-to-day implications of love and service. But Jesus wants the whole of us.

Our daily lives included.

24. Feminism as a Subversive Activity or Some Thoughts on Men's Liberation

Women know more about living and serving than men do. They wash the dishes, they clean the toilets, they ferry the kids around, they make the beds.

Women are the servants—men have seen to that.

In these days of women's liberation things are changing (a little, anyway). Men are learning (a little, anyway) about washing dishes and cleaning toilets. And that's good: We're learning to serve (a little, anyway).

This is what it means to follow Jesus in the humdrum of daily life. It's not dramatic—it's just washing the dumb dishes.

Men washing dishes is generally called women's liberation. But I wonder if it shouldn't be called men's liberation. I think it's the men who are being set free, set free to serve.

And I worry a little about the women. I wonder if they aren't getting sucked into a rat race—the very rat race Jesus spoke so vehemently against. They're struggling to get into the work place on the same terms as men. And they certainly should have the same rights as men: There's no reason why men should be the bosses and women should be the secretaries—at a fraction of the wage.

But the rights that men have are not so wonderful. Remember that in the upside-down kingdom secretaries are more blessed than bosses. The great are those who serve, and tripling your wage isn't as big a gain as we suppose.

I have a young friend who is a genius at physics. She spent a summer working among the poor, and she decided to abandon physics because it had nothing to do with people. I was delighted (though not quite convinced). But when she decided to become a nurse, I was appalled. With her brains, I thought she should become a doctor at least. And I told her so. But according to her, doctors don't have much more contact with people than mathematicians do; they just write prescriptions on an assembly line.

I felt like arguing that doctors don't have to dehumanize patients in that way, that with the greater knowledge she'd have as a doctor she could serve more effectively. But I didn't say much. I suspected that I had too much of the wisdom of the world—that this young woman, this little child, knew more about the kingdom of God than I, with all my theological and political knowledge. By instinct she knew more about liberation than all the books on the subject I had ever read.

Dan Berrigan works as a volunteer on a ward for people with terminal cancer. With his brains, he could be more effective going back to school and researching a cure for cancer. (He could certainly earn a lot more.) But who would hold the hand of the sick as they died?

That's what it means to follow Jesus day to day: washing the dishes, becoming a nurse instead of a doctor, holding the hand of the dying. And men are learning that (at least a little) from women.

I hope women don't forget it themselves.

Feminism can take two directions. It can try to make men more like women, or it can try to make women more like men. At least in our culture, the ideal is for men to be hard and tough—in charge. For women, the ideal is to be compassionate and tender—servants.

One direction feminism can take is to encourage women to become hard and tough, to claim the male "ideal." Let's call that *taskmaster feminism*. The other direction is to encourage men to become soft and tender—to become servants as in the female ideal. Let's call that *servant feminism*.

Men are supposed to be strong, pushy, and success-oriented. We're not supposed to be interested in kids, nor are we supposed to be emotional. (Crying is especially forbidden, and tenderness is suspect.) Under the right circumstances, violence is a badge of honor (at war, in the boxing ring, or when your wife's "honor" is at stake).

Women are supposed to be weak, tender, and home-oriented. They're expected to cry, to be interested in kids, and to clean up other people's messes. It's okay for them to lack that little extra spark of drive needed to "make it" in the competitive world.

Needless to say I lean toward servant feminism. Especially for men.

Of course, I do not mean that men should become like our culture's stereotype of women. I do not believe that passivity is a virtue for men or women. Nor is it a virtue for anyone to live up to our culture's expectation of women as irrational, empty-headed, or interested only in trivia like the fall fashions.

With those (substantial) exceptions, I think men need to become more like the ideal for women—not the other way around. Servant feminism is on the right track.

It's also peculiarly like the teaching of Jesus.

I do not mean you can give a proof text showing that Jesus preferred "servant" qualities to those of the taskmaster, but I do think Jesus' whole teaching points in that direction.

His teaching about serving two masters and laying up treasures decisively undercuts success orientation, and so does what he says about taking up your cross. His rebuke of the disciples for keeping children away from him would be easier for us to understand if he had been a woman.

And how can Jesus' statement about turning the other cheek be squared with the way little boys are encouraged to defend themselves and their honor with violence. It's a wonder little boys grow up to be human at all given the daily fare of tough guys on TV.

Think of the Beatitudes. In Luke's version, Jesus blesses the poor, the hungry, and those who weep. That hardly sounds like praise for tough centurions or those who have succeeded in the corporate world.

And if weeping is an ideal for Jesus, why do we discourage men from doing it? Or are the Beatitudes only for women?

In Matthew's version, Jesus blesses the poor in spirit, the mourners, the meek (probably best translated as the gentle), the merciful, and the peacemakers. Mourners and the merciful sound a little emotional, and peacemakers and the gentle don't sound like they'd make it on a professional football team.

The picture Jesus paints as the ideal is scarcely that of a tough, hard man. It's someone softer, gentler, with more feeling—more like our culture's ideal of a woman. Jesus would prefer nurses to bosses. His ideal is compassionate servanthood.

The problem is, some feminist women are not being servants. After all, they've been washing dishes and doing men's typing for an awfully long time, and they're tired of it. Obviously, women must make that choice themselves. In a culture where women are made to be servants, they can scarcely choose to follow Jesus into servanthood: The choice has already been made for them, and so is not a real commitment.

But we must be clear: We all have the right to choose. Once we claim that right, we must choose to be servants, not bosses. I believe myself that the desire to be a boss is similar to the desire of many in concentration camps to be like their guards. Some oppressed people always think that liberation means being strong enough to be the one who does the oppressing. But liberation is ending the oppression and transcending the oppressor's values.

Not seeing that, many blacks copy whites, the children of immigrants reject their parents' culture, poor people usually want to be rich, revolutionaries who overthrow dictators regularly become dictators themselves—and many women want to become bosses.

But Christians are called to "women's work."

And that's subversive.

For years, the religious right has argued that feminism threatens to corrupt Western values and to undermine American institutions. I have never understood their concern; I thought they were just afraid of change. But increasingly I suspect that they are correct. Feminism, at least in its servant form, is profoundly subversive.

What would happen if a servant mind-set permeated our culture? If people just weren't so concerned about success? If our need to bash our enemies' faces lessened? (What if a company advertised for a boss, and no one applied? What if they held a war, and . . . .) No wonder the right is alarmed. The very foundations of our culture are being challenged by feminism. A cultural revolution is threatening.

What if Exxon had a woman president and board of directors? Mightn't they be nearly as concerned about service as profits? About employees as stockholders? What if half the recruits in the Marines were women, and they just wouldn't do the crazy things they were told to do? What if they laughed when told to sleep with their rifles?

One of the most encouraging things I know about is the gender gap in voting. Women are less supportive of Reagan than are men. It's not that they are more likely to support the Equal Rights Amendment. (In fact, more men support it than women.) But women are more likely to disagree with Reagan and other men on issues of force—gun control, the death penalty, nuclear weapons. The gap is as great as 20 percent.

The religious right has something to worry about.

Servant feminists challenge our whole culture. They are calling for new values—ones that undermine the old order. Servant feminism isn't glamorous, and it doesn't pay very well, but it sure beats being the boss.

They who lose their lives shall find them.

25. Words: An Aside on Terminology

But what shall we call this different sort of life?

I've never liked the term *simple living.* It gives too much emphasis to economics when Jesus called us to a whole way of life. Besides, let's face it: simple living isn't simple. In fact, it's quite complicated.

It's harder to hang your clothes out than to throw them in the dryer. Walking to the co-op and doing your job as a working member takes longer than driving to the supermarket and shopping. Gardening bores me, and the communal car is always breaking down. And what's so simple about rehabilitating an abandoned house?

They told me communal living would simplify things. There'd be four people to fix the roof instead of just me.

And four people to fight with, too. But no one told me that.

The meetings were endless.

And the roof never leaked.

Mind you, that's not the whole story. Standard suburban living isn't so simple either. Earning enough to maintain two cars, a freezer, a dryer, a color TV, membership in the Y, and a power mower takes time. By the time you've also bought life insurance, car insurance (on two cars), health insurance, and contributed to your I.R.A., you can't make it on one salary. You really can't. You still have to pay city tax, state tax, income tax, unemployment insurance, and social security.

I'd take my present way of life anytime. I can't stand those Saturday afternoons at the shopping mall. And keeping track of how wide my tie and trouser bottoms should be this year just isn't my thing. Simple living *is* liberating.

So the normal American way of life is probably even more complicated than simple living. But don't start living simply because you think it's going to be simple. For that you need a housekeeper, a gardener, a bookkeeper, a body servant—and a million dollars.

Now *that's* simple living.

But it isn't Christian.

The term *simple living*, despite its inadequacies, does point to how Christians are to have only one goal. "Seek first the kingdom of heaven and God's righteousness." The kingdom is our goal, and we shouldn't be distracted by other goals like money or status. Grasping that point does simplify our lives. We're freed from the concerns of the world. And that's great.

But the term *simple living* doesn't capture that point very clearly. To most people it just means spending less, which is crucial, but it's not the heart of the matter. So I'm inclined to stop talking about simple living.

Maybe *voluntary poverty* is a better phrase.

One small problem is that we aren't poor. Maybe Jesus, St. Francis, and Gandhi were poor, but we aren't. Compared to the average American, we may seem poor or we may even be under the poverty line set by the government. But we aren't poor. I know only one or two people who are genuinely poor by choice.

The only time I ever went hungry for lack of money was in college when I hitchhiked around Europe. That's how people live who talk about voluntary poverty.

People who are poor can't get medical care for their kids. And that's different.

What's more, voluntary poverty is a contradiction in terms. The essence of poverty is not having control of your own life, not having choices. If you choose poverty, you can almost always choose to get out. And that means you're not poor—you're just broke.

Which is different.

So what name should we use for this way of life? The term doesn't matter much, but we need to be clear what our calling is. And sometimes I'm afraid we're not.

Part of the calling is not using more than our share of the world's resources. That's only fair, and it's important. (Maybe we should call it *living fairly*.)

Part of it is sharing with the needy. It's obscene to live so luxuriously when people are starving. (Maybe we should call it *living justly*.)

A bigger part of the calling is seeing through the tinsel façade of American life. Then we will find that people count more than consumption. We will find the spring of living water; possessions and self-importance will fade. Then we will be free. (Maybe we should call it *more-with-less living* or *living free*.)

Another big part of the calling is learning to trust God instead of possessions. God wants us to learn that possessions aren't reliable. God is going to take care of us; our insurance policies aren't. (Maybe we should call it *trustful living*.)

Another part of the calling is serving others, especially the oppressed. That's going to mean living on little. Nobody will pay us much to do it, and the going will get rough. That will force us to trust God. And to find springs of living water. Otherwise we'll burn out and quit. It's going to be a hassle. Being available, loving people, being a servant, fighting oppression—those are what count.

I think we should call it *servant living*.

26. Assertiveness

You've probably heard about the couple who went to the movies every Saturday night. Both of them hated it, but neither knew the other did. Each went to please the other.

You might call it servant living.

But mostly it was stupid.

And according to the wisdom of the world, so was Jesus. The way most psychologists tell it, turning the other cheek is a model of how not to respond to conflict. Unless we're out fighting for our rights and demanding what we want, we'll never find fulfillment. We'll be angry people who take our aggressions out passively: If we go with someone to a movie when we don't want to, we'll ruin it for the other person by making fun of the acting or arriving late for the show—which is dishonest and manipulative as well as hostile. Only assertive, fulfilled people can be kind and loving. Or so I'm told.

And there's a lot to that analysis.

Feminists have helped make the importance of assertiveness clear, and it has been a revelation to me. Many women (and a few men) are so concerned about what other people want that they don't know what they want themselves. They lose track of who they are and become frustrated and angry. By the time they get what they want, they're too angry to enjoy it. In no time, they're victims waiting for someone to hit them on the other cheek. They refuse to accept responsibility for their own lives and blame others for the mess they're making. People need to take charge of their lives.

But on the other hand, assertiveness tends to leave us preoccupied with ourselves. And we get sucked into narcissism. So you find people in their thirties still drifting because they haven't found fulfilling work. And people get abortions because a child wouldn't be fulfilling at that point in their lives. And marriages end because someone gets bored.

What do we do here? Do we accept assertiveness training whole hog and ignore Jesus? (No need to say he was wrong; just don't notice what he said.) Do we reject assertiveness training out-of-hand and wind up with a bunch of passive-aggressive malcontents? No, we measure assertiveness training against what Jesus taught to see if maybe we misunderstood him.

Whatever Jesus was, he wasn't passive. He seemed to positively court confrontation with the Pharisees. When he spoke to them, he spoke assertively. He hit them right between the eyes. Jesus didn't dither; he knew his own mind. When speaking to people, he didn't first find out what they wanted to hear and then tailor his words to please them. Ask the rich young ruler.

We think that turning the other cheek means acting like dishrags. But turning the other cheek is not passive; it's assertive. Passivity is doing nothing. It's letting things collapse around your ears while you procrastinate, pretending nothing is wrong. It's following the path of least resistance.

But turning the other cheek is a long way from the path of least resistance. (Try it sometime, and you'll find out.) It's decisive action, and that's assertive.

Neither does turning the other cheek imply accepting abuse silently. It is quite compatible with telling others that they are abusing you. Thus when an officer struck Jesus, Jesus did not strike back, but neither did he keep quiet: He told the soldier clearly that he had no right to lay a finger on him (John 18:23).

Sometimes we think being a servant means being passive, but that is not necessarily true. Jesus washed the disciples' feet—an assertive act. Then he asked Judas to leave—a very assertive act. He served the sick by healing them, but he healed them even on the Sabbath, knowing how that would infuriate the Pharisees. (He didn't whisper to the sick to meet him around the corner where no one would see.)

And above all, Jesus was not manipulative. When he was exhausted from dealing with the crowd, he told them so and left. (See, for example, Mark 4:35–38.) He didn't claim to have a headache that made him not feel like being with them just then. Nor did he blame the crowd for his headache; it was *his* choice to be with them. He was not a victim—not even at Golgotha.

Jesus knew himself. He knew his limits. He was assertive— an assertive servant.

And we should be, too.

Assertive servanthood. That is what Jesus calls us to.

But what does that mean? Suppose your church is choosing a new pastor or elder. Assertive servanthood means you state your views forthrightly and maybe even vigorously. But if the decision doesn't go your way, you support the new person anyway (except in most unusual cases). And you don't brood over it or become bitter about it. (Especially if the person not chosen is yourself.)

That requires you to know yourself well enough to realize what you want and why. It requires you to serve the new person. It means not trying to manipulate the decision ahead of time but allowing people room to act as they really believe. You're not trying to get your way but to let the wisdom of the group and the guidance of the Spirit emerge. (You might learn something yourself.)

And afterwards you aren't to be abusive to those who disagree (even if you're confident that the choice wasn't the best). And you certainly aren't to repress your anger but to deal with it openly and honestly. (Whatever that means.)

And at home? What is assertive servanthood there? It is washing the dumb dishes and cleaning the bathroom—doing the boring jobs and the dirty ones, the ones others don't want to do. But if you turn out to be doing more than your share of work, or maybe of dirty work, you make that clear. You may keep doing it, but you tell people what you think is happening—without playing the whining martyr.

At mealtimes, you shouldn't be much more likely than anyone else to get up for more water or a serving spoon (or much *less* likely, either). Everyone needs to learn to pull their own weight, especially men and kids. Make sure you do. Then be assertive that others do the same. (Keeping a count of who naturally gets up most at mealtimes is a good way to tell who is the servant in the house.)

And when you're the one dividing treats, don't give yourself the biggest and the best. Give them to the kids; maybe they'll learn to be generous.

In our home, dividing up the housework has always been a problem. We're all too busy. We don't have problems over who does the dirty work, I'm glad to say, but we do have problems over who should do how much. Much of that has grown out of not being assertive enough. We've had trouble being clear about our needs, wants, and limits—sometimes because we haven't been clear about them with ourselves.

When we haven't been clear, we've gotten abusive. Which is quite different from being assertive.

And that gets us back to turning the other cheek, which I think is about not being abusive. We're to accept abuse without being abusive. Jesus responded to the officer who struck him, but he didn't abuse him. (I'm not so sure he didn't abuse the Pharisees when they abused him, but I presume his reaction was righteous indignation.)

The point is, we're not to return tit for tat. But that does not mean we are required to be passive. We can speak up, fairly and perhaps kindly. We do not have to choose between abusiveness and passivity, and it is an indication of our spiritual poverty that we think we do.

How is assertive servanthood different from the wisdom of the world? The difference is in being a servant, but not kidding yourself about what you're doing. I think the whining comes with the dishonesty—not saying what we want, or worse, not knowing. The problem isn't so much with the serving as with kidding ourselves about it. Jesus was clear that he didn't want to be crucified, and I suspect that made it easier for him to proceed without anger and whining.

Suppose you and someone else are considering going to that movie. First off, both of you have to know and say what you want. And if you want different things, then presumably you do different things. Or else you be creative and find something else you both want to do. (That's assertiveness training.)

But what if the other person really wants you to come along, and it doesn't seem to be a power play? For example, my daughter once wanted me to take her to a Muppet movie that I had no interest in seeing. She was too young to go by herself, so we tried to find someone else to take her. But we couldn't find anyone, so I finally took her. I didn't enjoy the movie (to say the least), but that little bit of serving didn't hurt me any.

This brings me to what is dangerous about assertiveness training. In its worst forms, it seems to claim no one should do anything that isn't completely and utterly fulfilling to them. And that's at least as silly as a couple going to a movie every Saturday night for years when neither wanted to. You have to spend a fair amount of life doing things that are at least mildly unpleasant. Otherwise you're a spoiled brat who will never accomplish anything fulfilling because some of the steps on the way aren't exciting. And you'll never maintain a relationship because some unpleasant serving always needs to be done. (Hence the high divorce rate, though lack of assertiveness contributes its share, too.) The unwillingness to accept the unpleasant seems to me to be a central failing of our culture.

But what about the difficult cases? What if your spouse demands that you go to a movie, and you think your spouse is merely trying to control you? What does an assertive servant do then? I think you sometimes go. Other times you may serve your spouse better by not going (if the demand is part of a pathology or the person needs to be shaken awake—or would one of those always be the case?).

But I fear we have to suffer wrong sometimes. Peter's teaching must apply to our lives occasionally, or we're playing hypocritical games. Peter says these jarring words:

Servants, be submissive to your masters with all respect, not only to the kind and gentle but also to the overbearing. For to this you have been called, because Christ also suffered for you, leaving you an example, that you should follow in his steps. When he was reviled, he did not revile in turn; when he suffered, he did not threaten. (1 Pet. 2:18, 21, 23)

But the idea of accepting suffering is foreign to me and my culture. And even more foreign to some of today's liberation movements. I'm more at home with self-fulfillment. I'm in no hurry to get crucified.

But I suspect that the need for self-fulfillment is one of the chief delusions of our age—one of our chief principalities and powers. It keeps us from the suffering and weakness that could maim the forces of evil.

They that lose their lives save them.

27. Jobs and Kingdom Work

Many of us devote half our waking hours to things connected with our work. Whatever we may say our priorities are, our time and energy are devoted to our jobs. So if the kingdom is first in our lives, our work will be kingdom work.

Given the mess that the world is in—the poor kids dying, the people being tortured, the nearly universal spiritual death—you'd think we'd want to devote our energies to spreading life. But our work is a ghetto that most of us have not even considered bringing under the Lordship of Jesus Christ. We may give a tithe, even a graduated tithe, but we rarely give our lives or even our jobs.

Meanwhile the church gives us little guidance on what kingdom work is. It does not often challenge us in bad work or support us in good work.

So what does servant living mean when it comes to jobs?

Maybe it's my fundamentalist background, but I still think we're all called to full-time Christian service. Not that we have to work for the church, but whatever we do, it should fully serve God and God's creation—especially people and most especially poor and hurting people.

What that means for specific jobs, I often don't know, but I am clear on some general principles. Perhaps the most obvious of these principles is that pay is irrelevant. The work we do should not be chosen by how well it pays. Jesus was clear that we should be about the business of the kingdom and let God take care of our money.

Yet clergy refuse churches that don't pay well enough, some Christians become lawyers solely to make money, and corporate executives accept raises for being transferred to new cities even when it means leaving a solid church for an unknown church.

Obviously people who are working for their own wealth (or power) are wasting themselves and their lives. And such things are the mainsprings of an awful lot of work. So we can say right off that the enormous part of work life governed by such tinsel is dead wrong. As Christians we must reject that kind of motivation out of hand. Kingdom work is elsewhere. We have better things to do.

An equally important principle is that we must think of our jobs structurally. Some Christians are doubtless getting rich selling Chiquita bananas, and a couple of them are probably trying to live simply so that they can give money for relief in "banana republics." The catch is that the money they make off bananas depends on underpaying the workers, farmers, and sometimes the governments of the banana republics. And it means devoting less land to growing food that poor local people can eat. So their relief money is going to relieve the exploiting they do; it allows them to feel good about exploiting others. They are returning as charity what they got by stealing. And that is worse than awful.

So we cannot devote our lives to increasing the profits of companies that live off exploitation. We must think about economic and political structures in ways that we usually don't. Does export cropping do harm? How much pesticide and cotton dust should workers be exposed to? Does our company make significant profits by bamboozling poor people into buying products they don't need? Is the company fair about unions? Do they invest in South Africa?

I suspect that more harm is done by good people quietly doing their jobs for such groups and doing them well than by all the crime and malice in the world. If the faceless bureaucrats, the cogs in the machines, the people who do the daily work—if they'd rise up and say No, who knows what change might be produced.

I'm also clear that we should avoid jobs that deal in death.

Christians can't design or help manufacture bigger and better bombs. Only slightly less serious is growing and selling tobacco for people to kill themselves with. And speaking of food, I wonder how many Christians spend their lives manufacturing and selling ever-less-nutritious junk food?

I'm clear too that Christians shouldn't trade on false values. Many products rely on appeals to status, false sex, and other nonsense. Christians can't spend themselves designing, making, advertising, or selling such trash. Fashions, sexy cars, Barbie dolls, things to make you look younger or richer—we cannot be in such businesses. Nor can we be in businesses that help useful products pretend to be sexy or high status. (Notice toothpaste ads.)

Nor should we tolerate polluting God's creation. We cannot be dumping destructive chemicals into the water, or eating up more land with shopping malls so that we can have more things we don't need.

But this is all abstract. The issues are more difficult when we deal with concrete cases. Should a Christian work for United Brands (the Chiquita banana people)? Can a person be a servant there? Given their record of exploitation in Central America, what is a Christian to do? (Similar questions could be asked of pastoring a church, being a politician, teaching in the public school system, joining a law firm, or being a social worker. But I'm only going to ask it of United Brands.)

Perhaps the question has no right answer. The best I can say, other than give my prejudices, is that if Christians work for United Brands, they should be there to do good. If they are on a policy-making level, they should be pushing for higher wages for Third World workers, fighting for fairer contracts for farmers, and trying to hire more minority workers in the United States. (I am less clear what to say about the job of a United Brands warehouse worker.)

Personally I doubt that the company would tolerate such a person for long. But I could be wrong; I don't have any experience in such companies. However I do have a lot of experience in Christian agencies, and I know that few of them can handle such stances. So unless United Brands is better than Christian agencies (which is possible), they would probably quickly fire such a person.

But my purpose is not to get people driven out of their jobs; it is to get them to ask the right questions. If Christians working for United Brands can say with integrity that they are increasing justice, feeding more people, or decreasing pollution, then fine. Certainly people in key positions in industry have a chance, for example, to provide more employment for minorities than all of us do-gooders combined. But I do not see this kind of action taking place. I do not even see these people asking the right questions.

What such people must ask is whether they are living by kingdom values. Are they following Jesus or being co-opted by United Brands? Is reality for them basically determined by the Sermon on the Mount or by the pressure of their job? I hate to be judgmental, but I fear I know the answer in most cases. We cannot serve God and mammon.

Yet all of this is too cautious. I am asking what kind of work is allowed, and that is the wrong tone. It is like the teenagers asking how far they can go. The question doesn't go nearly deep enough. We shouldn't ask what jobs are allowed, but where we can make the greatest contribution.

My main concern about jobs is not that people are doing bad things as much as that they are doing pointless things. The world is going to hell around our ears, and we are helping manufacture soap to get rid of "ring around the collar." We are selling iceboxes on the burning deck.

Instead of frittering away our time and talent making an irrelevant company more profitable, we should be doing work that helps. I cannot understand why Christians are wasting their lives when so much needs to be done.

Part of the problem here is mind-set. We assume that most

Christians will get jobs at the supermarket, as corporate lawyers, or on an assembly line. We think it's sensible to help make stuff to put in dryers to prevent static cling. A handful of half-saints get personal calls to serve God and people. We respect, in a way, those who leave secular jobs for such service, but they are a breed apart.

Yet that is the reverse of the case. We are called to serve God and people. That is the only job that any of us really has. It takes no special call from beyond. The only question is whether we have sought a place of service. In some cases, someone might get a call to fight for justice as an executive of United Brands, but I suspect that *they* are the breed apart. I suspect that they are the ones who should wait for a special call, for a voice from God.

Underlying all this is a trap. We tend too easily to calculate effectiveness. That prompts us to set out to be president of United Brands, to aim as "high" as we can. We instinctively believe that the more power and prestige we have, the more good we can do. I'll call this the success view.

The opposite position is that power and prestige are ephemeral, corrupting, and irrelevant. The way you help people is not to use power but to be a servant—to empty bedpans, to do the dirty work no one else wants to do . . . to do women's work. I'll call this the servant view.

The success view certainly makes sense on the surface. You pick a profession, get the best (or possibly the most prestigious) credentials you can, and work your way up the ladder of success. On your way up (or at least when you get to the top), you help poor and hurting people.

But in my experience, people who strive for power or money to help the poor make awfully good use of that money and power—for themselves. Getting into the success game is almost sure to have you lying to yourself half the time.

Besides, I know what it ordinarily takes to succeed. You have to endlessly scratch the right backs, dress right (remember those books on dressing for success?), keep quiet when you shouldn't. You have to tell the bosses they're great when they aren't and ignore the important things while you strive for your goal of success.

I also think we tend to take ourselves and our jobs too seriously. Although we should be looking for jobs that will help, we shouldn't kid ourselves about how much good we're doing. I know many academics who think their work has enduring value, but the fact is that most academic treatises (not to mention my own writing) are forgotten almost before they are written. The lasting value of most scholars rests not on their scholarship but on how they relate to their students.

I wonder whether we have understood the depths of the gospel. In our heart of hearts, don't we believe that the way to kill Goliath is to become as much like him as possible? (While giving God the glory, of course.) But it was the kid David who killed Goliath, not a clone of Goliath.

Instead of seizing the gospel call to servant living, haven't we seized the American dream of success and effectiveness? Not that it's always wrong to be effective, but effectiveness is never the final criterion. Love and faithfulness are what count.

Our commitment to effectiveness is really a denial that sin is the root of our problems. Down deep we expect technological solutions to our problems. We believe that the doctor, with sophisticated technology, is the one to deal with human suffering. But that reflects a very shallow understanding of suffering. In fact, it reflects a shallow understanding of illness. As is becoming increasingly clear, even our illnesses often have spiritual roots. And everything else has spiritual roots, too.

And Goliaths, even Goliaths born again at Billy Graham rallies, are not equipped for spiritual warfare.

In *Voyage of the Dawn Treader*, by C. S. Lewis, one of the characters says, "In our world, a star is a huge ball of flaming gas." Another person replies, "That is not what a star is but only what it is made of."[1] That is similar to how we respond when someone asks us what we do. We reply that we're electricians or editors, when our jobs are only what our lives are made of. What we *do* is meditate on beauty (or on our own prestige), love our kids (or get too busy to notice them), serve our neighbors and colleagues (or try to get them to serve us).

If we finally grasp what to do with our lives, then the rest will fall into place.

Recently I heard a retired ballerina being interviewed about her early career. She talked with enthusiasm about the hard work, the long hours, the low pay for herself and her friends. They were paid so little they didn't always have as much to eat as they'd have liked. The interviewer commented that it was really a shame it had been so tough. She looked at him blankly for a moment, as if something were wrong with him. Then she said something like, "Oh, no. We were doing what we were meant to do, what we wanted to do. The lack of money and the hard work were irrelevant. We were dancing."

She knew what she was doing with her life, and that made everything else fall into place. Her response is a common one among artists. They paint, act, write, or whatever. Their only question is how to hold body and soul together while they do it. How will they finance their art? It is common to find them driving taxis or washing dishes to pay the rent, but their life is their art. Art is what they are about.

I wonder why Christians aren't as consumed by what they do? How many Christians have you known so hooked on fighting for justice that they wash dishes to finance their habit? Or so excited by worship that they drive a taxi nights so they can pray and meditate all day?

Notice how money falls into place the way artists look at things. Money is merely a tool to further their work. If they can sell their art without too much loss of integrity, fine. It's easier that way. But if they can't, they find a job to finance their real work. They become tentmakers. For them living on a little is not a principle; it's just what they do to practice their art. They've no time to make money. Art is their vocation; their job is only a pastime.

A long time ago I was struck by something about most Christians who choose to live on a little. Few of them use the rhetoric of simple living—or even believe it. But they have found a ministry that consumes their lives. They have no time to earn money, and no one will pay them well for their work. So they get along on a little, almost without noticing it, so they can do their work.

They have found the pearl of great price. They have found kingdom work. The debates, rhetoric, and hard questions are irrelevant. The excitement seizes them.

Find your work. Then your job will take care of itself. And so will money. Everything will fall into place. "Seek first the kingdom of God and God's righteousness, and all these things shall be yours as well."

Then you can say, "Oh, we're doing what we're meant to do. We're dancing."

28. Model One: Will the Real Alligator Please Stand Up?

How then should we live when it comes to money? I hesitate to be too specific; I'd rather leave things in turmoil the way Jesus did. I won't give any rules. Instead I'll point to some models—models that in some ways come close to the way of Jesus and in some ways do not.

The Thoreau model is my favorite. I hate plastic, and I love God's creation. I'd like to trade the rat race for nature.

One year a speaking engagement took me near both Glacier National Park and Disney World. Glacier is one of the wonders of God's creation: lakes, mountain passes, hundreds of bald eagles, glaciers, streams. In one valley, gnarled trees grow at a forty-five-degree angle because of the ferocious prevailing wind. There fifteen bighorn sheep blocked us in while they ate flowers by the car. At another place a sign read, "Display ahead." It was a place where you could park your car and look out at the mountains which were beyond imagining.

Glacier is real.

Disney World is imitation. There is a boat ride on an imitation jungle river with alligators opening their mouths wide as if to eat you. Except the alligators are plastic.

There is not one real thing in the whole park (unless it's the roller coaster which really takes your stomach). Oh, and the horses that pull the trolleys—they're real. Each one is followed by a person who sweeps up its droppings as they hit the ground. Mustn't let anyone step in reality.

A popular ride is the grand prix. On it you race a car along a guided track at five or ten miles an hour. Great for the kids, of course. But I saw adults standing in line there for twenty minutes, and not all of them had kids with them. Some I'm sure had driven to Disney World at sixty miles an hour.

So what's the attraction?

Who wants plastic imitations when you can have the real thing?

Most people, apparently. Certainly my son. I told him he could join me on one of my trips, and, of course, he chose the trip to Florida so he could see Disney World. He didn't choose Montana.

He was not alone. Disney World was so full you could hardly move. The economy of central Florida revolves around this amusement park. Other amusement parks and hundreds of hotels have grown up around it. An expressway leads to it: four lanes exit at Disney World and two go on. I saw tour groups from England, Germany, and Japan.

Meanwhile Glacier is served by a two-lane road. A couple of towns are nearby, but their whole populations could fit into one of the Disney hotels. And the only thing revolving around Glacier is eagles. The closest thing I saw to a tour group was two carloads of Brownies watching the eagles feed on salmon.

Maybe I'm just a snob. Maybe I've lost the excitement of childhood. (Certainly the multitudes and the kids don't feel as I do; maybe I'm a Pharisee.) Maybe Disney World is one of humanity's great creations, like Chartres Cathedral or the paintings of Rembrandt.

But I doubt it. I don't think Disney World even has good imitations.

It frightens me that an overwhelming majority of people prefer imitations. We do not have wooden tables anymore; we have plastic tables with imitation wood grain. (I'm writing on one.) Maybe it's only a question of aesthetics, but I cannot believe that beauty is unrelated to truth and goodness. Plastic entertainment and plastic tables tie in with plastic living, plastic truth, and plastic virtue.

I wonder if our preference for imitations sets us up to prefer television evangelists to the message of Jesus? If you aren't bored by a plastic alligator, you won't be bored by a plastic preacher. Or offended by a plastic politician.

But most of us have poor reality detectors. We prefer not to know when faced with plastic and lies. We don't want to step in reality. Unable to tell the difference between margarine and butter, we believe that nuclear war won't happen, that the United States is fighting to save those forty thousand kids, that Jesus didn't mean for *us* to sell our possessions. We are studiedly inexperienced at finding truth.

And we are also studiedly inexperienced at spotting beauty. If we cut ourselves off from the horror of kids starving, I wonder if we don't also cut ourselves off from the beauty of little wild flowers and from the wonder of the gospel. If we won't look into the chasms, won't we also miss the peaks?

As Keats has said, Truth and beauty—and I would add goodness—are one.[1]

So I think it's important to find a way of life that isn't plastic. We need to get rid of Cuisinart food processors that take longer to clean than it would take to chop the carrots by hand. I won't eat TV dinners, peaches out of a can, or gourmet processed cheese. Vegetables from the garden are better than the supermarkets' (especially the tomatoes), and nothing compares to hand-packed all-natural ice cream, unless it's young corn hand-picked moments before and boiled for two minutes.

That kind of living not only gets you closer to God's world—to reality—but it can also cost less. You can get rid of all the plastic geegaws and silly appliances. A half-empty house is cheaper to furnish and quicker to clean. A wooden table needn't cost more, and it'll probably last longer. If you have a quarter of the clothes others have, think how much less storage space you'll need. And somehow the real reaches deeper than plastic and lessens the lure of success, money, and neon. With so much less mess, it's easier to find what you're looking for—whether it's your shoes or your soul.

But in the meantime I live in the Germantown section of Philadelphia. It's not a slum (at least, not anymore), but it's a long way from Montana. I hate the wrappers and broken glass strewn all over Pulaski Avenue. But at least we have a park about a block away. It's not Glacier, but it's okay. It's cut in half by an expressway, and the birds are mainly grackles and pigeons—*very* few eagles.

But why don't we move to Glacier or Walden Pond? I'm convinced that that's how God intended us to live; such places are pale reflections of the Garden of Eden. But at the Fall we chose another life, and now we are at war. As a result, serving the oppressed and resisting the powers of evil are crucial now, and that is quite different from living in the Garden of Eden. Living near Glacier and eating hand-packed ice cream have to take a back seat to fighting oppression. Loving and serving is our primary call.

You can do that in Montana, of course, and maybe someday I will. But where you live, how much beauty you have around you, is not the primary issue. How you can serve is more important. And most of us can do that better in Germantown.

Yet Thoreau was almost right. His vision was close to God's ideal. That accounts for the power of the idea of returning to nature. It's right out of Genesis and Isaiah. (It also accounts for the fallacy of the belief that simple living requires grubby living.)

But baptizing Thoreau is not enough. We must also put him in the back seat. For we are on a war footing, a war against evil and oppression. The front seat is living as servants.

Refusing to live for beauty doesn't mean we have to surround ourselves with plastic junk. Or prefer imitation alligators. Or launder "dry clean only" clothes. Or watch bad television. If we do those things, we're cutting ourselves off from reality. We're missing some of God's great gifts.

After all, Thoreau was almost right. Truth and beauty—and goodness—are one. Almost.

29. Model Two: On Being Cheap

Once I spoke at a conference on simple living. Someone asked the usual question: "But how do you *do* it?" I heard myself reply: "Easy. Just be cheap."

For most of us, money does a disappearing act. We don't want to be rich, but leading a half-decent life by American standards somehow costs twenty-five or thirty thousand dollars a year. Money runs between our fingers, and we don't even have much plastic junk to show for it. It's just gone. While people in the Third World survive on a few hundred dollars a year, we sincerely say that we're barely making it on twenty-five thousand. And the poor, whom we care about, aren't fed.

If we'd learn to manage our money better (if we'd learn to be cheap), our salaries would go twice as far. If we could live on five, ten, or fifteen thousand a year, we could serve in many more ways.

So frugality is my second model for servant living. And like the Thoreau model it's only partly right.

So I've worried about my advice to be cheap ever since. It can't have been right. Jesus never told us to be cheap—he never even hinted at it. But that's not all that worries me.

It also worries me that I was giving a technical answer to what I believe is a moral problem. I was talking about money management which is a technique.

And I was partly right.

Not all of our problems are moral and spiritual; some of them, or some aspects of them, are technical and technological. As a result, when you break your arm, you go first to a doctor, not to a minister. Of course, your broken arm may have a moral dimension: You may have broken it in a drunken driving accident or in military combat. So both the technical and the moral aspects of the problem need to be addressed.

And that's the way it is with money, too.

Careful money management is a mind-set. And I'm not talking about whether to invest in the stock market or in an IRA. I'm talking about how to feed one person on fifteen dollars a week instead of on forty. I'm not going to approach this question by listing a whole series of practical steps (eat more beans and less meat). Rather I'm going to talk about a mind-set.

The mind-set is not to spend money. It's that simple. The mind-set is related to the old line about Christians having more money because they don't spend it on wine, women, and song. Only the list is longer. You don't spend it on coffee and donuts, either. Or on Coke and potato chips. Or on new running shoes and the newspaper. Or on a new car and a color television set. You do without such irrelevancies.

I travel a lot, often with other people. I know their mind-set at once if they keep buying junk food. They're in trouble, and it doesn't matter how much they earn. If they spend money that way, they spend it all. On something. No matter how much they have.

I have a good friend whom I've known for years. He's not concerned about money; he's concerned about justice. When I first knew him, he was always broke. I thought it was because his income was low (which it was). But now he has a big income, and he's still broke. It's the cigarettes. And things like that. He'll always be broke.

You have to explain to yourself that you need hardly anything. And keep explaining it to yourself. Because we can persuade ourselves that we need almost everything. You don't need to drive all over town every day. You don't need another tie. You don't need that processed food from the grocery store. You don't need grapefruit spoons or a device to strip the corn off the cob. If you persuade yourself you need to go to a movie (frivolity is a necessity), go at a cheap time and take your own popcorn. My wife says we don't need a TV, but I claim it's cheaper than flying to the Superbowl. (At least I watch on a little, old battered black and white TV—unless I can get someone to invite me over who has a color set.)

What I'm saying is, manage your money carefully: stick to a budget, be hardheaded, and don't buy junk food. In other words, be cheap. That way you can live on half the national average. And live better, while serving a whole lot more.

Remember my friend who is always broke? I said it was the cigarettes. But that's not the whole story.

He's also generous. When I'm with him and he buys junk food, he always gets some for me, too. And he's not concerned enough about money to spend his time haunting sales or searching for second-hand clothes. He's a free spirit, which I admire.

I think I may be more materialistic than he is, and further from the spirit of Christ. I wonder if my mind-set doesn't owe as much to the spirit of capitalism as to the spirit of Christ. I wonder if all my calculating and scrimping and cutting corners doesn't leave me mired in the cares of this world. Jesus wanted us to trust God for money, but I scarcely need to—I manage quite well on my own. Jesus praised the poor widow for being generous, though she managed her money badly.

Yet I still think that careful money management is good. It's open to abuses, but it's basically sound. Careful money management is a form of economic discipline—something not popular in our hedonistic age. But it's vital nonetheless. We shouldn't be spending on every whim, especially not every whim sent by the principalities on Madison Avenue.

Economic discipline means finding what our needs are and then meeting them—not buying a bunch of excess trash. It's not a whole lot different from discipline elsewhere. Discipline in sleep means finding out how much sleep you need and then getting that much—not a whole lot less, not a whole lot more.

In our day, of course, people are liable to believe in follow-ing whims. If they feel like staying up late they do—anytime the "spirit" moves them. They think that doing this makes them free spirits, but all it does is make them tired. They're not free spirits; they're dopes. And the same is true of people who are always broke no matter how much they earn. The person who is free is the one with discipline.

Of course, discipline can get out of hand. Some people think discipline is finding out how much sleep you need and then seeing to it that you get less than that. But that's perverse. That's not discipline, it's asceticism.

A more common way for discipline to go awry in our day is for people to become consumed with whether they're going to get done on time, whether they're going to get enough sleep. It's called worrying—or insomnia. And that sort of thing can happen with money, too. Those trying to live on less can be-come consumed by it. They can get financially constipated.

You'll know money management has gotten out of hand if you spend all your energy gardening and visiting garage sales and have no time left for service. You'll know things have gone awry if you lose ten dollars and it ruins your day: money doesn't matter that much. You should wonder about yourself if you can never follow a whim to buy a marbled steak. And you'll know you've missed the point completely when you don't want to have guests over for dinner because it will ruin your food budget.

The discipline model has something to be said for it. Though it's not as good as the Thoreau model, it has its (limited) place. But don't let it run your life.

Be disciplined. But more important, be openhanded.

And don't be cheap.

30. Model Three: Going Part Way

Perhaps it's time for true confessions. Or even past time. I haven't sold all my possessions. Not by a long shot. And I have no intention of doing so.

You can't—it's not practical. How would you then live?

Oh, my family and I don't spend much.

We don't own a car. Most years we would even qualify for food stamps. In the last ten years, we've only bought one new piece of furniture (or maybe two). Our piano is a battered up-right, as old as I am. As much as I love professional foot-ball, I never go to a game; the tickets cost too much. We have no money saved for the kids to go to college. In fact, we have no savings to speak of: only a life insurance policy we bought when we didn't know any better, and we've borrowed on it almost to the hilt. We spend less on food than almost any American family I know except for a few who dumpster and garden—and we spend less than most of them.

On the unusual occasions when we tell people our income, they are almost always surprised that anyone can live on so little, even when they learn about the generous benefits that come with my job.

You see, we spend very little.

By American standards.

I feel quite heroic.

But we own our own house outright, and it's reasonably well furnished—not early Salvation Army. We have endless medical benefits and access to a company car. We go to lots of

Phillies games because grandstand seats are only $2.50 for adults and $1.00 for kids. And we do have life insurance, though it's only for $10,000.

Oh, and I have a couple thousand books (paperbacks, of course). Not to mention a half-decent stereo (old, naturally).

My family and I live quite extravagantly.

By any sane standards.

I feel quite silly.

What kind of world is it where you can say the grandstand costs *only* $2.50 when forty thousand kids will die today for want of that much money? It's crazy. Why does no one hiss when they hear the word *only* used that way? How can apparently sane people (namely me) use it like that? And then there's the life insurance for *only* $10,000.

Are we going to take Jesus seriously or not? Am *I* going to take Jesus seriously or not?

There are two options here. One is to install a device in your showerhead that reduces the amount of water used without reducing the pressure. (You wouldn't want to reduce the pressure, now would you?) Along with that go things like putting insulation in your attic, getting a wood stove (and cutting the wood yourself, of course), not replacing your furniture as it gets more and more worn (most houses are too crammed anyway), riding a bike (a ten-speed, of course), and installing solar heating.

If you're bright and dedicated, creative and disciplined—and not too generous—you can develop this option into a science, especially if your spouse is as good a money manager as mine. And then you're free to serve in quite a drastic way.

It's well worth doing, but it's not going all the way with Jesus. I, at least, haven't yet reached my limit. I haven't yet decided to go all the way home.

They say Gandhi could put all his possessions in a bag. I'm not sure that's the universal ideal, but it's a model of servant living that deserves consideration.

It's funny, isn't it. A Hindu doing what Jesus said, when Christians won't. We don't even consider it seriously.

And if we mention it as a possibility, other Christians hasten to assure us that it wouldn't work. It isn't practical. How would you *live?*

But Gandhi did it.

Probably it wasn't practical. But for a moment the world shook to its foundations.

It's our house that stops me. Both my wife and I worked for a couple years, and we saved a lot of money. We bought an inexpensive house and repaired it ourselves. The work hasn't made me all that attached to it (I hated it), but the plan was that owning a house would enable us to live on less and thereby do what we needed to do. And it has done that.

So I hesitate to sell it. Our house seems to me to be a weapon in the war against evil. Owning a house, or at least owning that house, is cheaper than renting an apartment. If we sold it and gave the money to the poor, we'd have to earn more—and probably serve less.

But most of the ways of saving money that I just mentioned aren't open to the genuinely poor. They don't have enough money to buy a house, install solar heating, or get a ten-speed bike. You have to have money to save money.

And I doubt that Jesus advocated saving up a nest egg so we could live more economically. I'm afraid he was advocating something more drastic—like getting rid of everything we can't fit in a bag.

I believe that Jesus' teaching on possessions—in fact, his whole life and ministry—were designed to demand a choice. Jesus wants us to choose. On the one hand are upward mobility, power, acceptability to family and friends, a comfortable life. On the other hand are weakness, suffering, God, and a bagful of possessions.

Jesus put so much emphasis on possessions because they are central in that choice. It's only a little bit of an exaggeration to say that it's money that makes the world go 'round; so Jesus wants us to make a decisive choice against money and its world. It's the desire for a comfortable life that leaves us indifferent, or at least inactive, in the face of kids starving and bombs being dropped.

So let's do more than put insulation in our attic. Let's get rid of so many of our possessions that we can fit all we have left in a bag. That will be servant living. And maybe the world will shake a little when someone chooses for God and against the world.

Now all I have to do is figure out how big a bag I'll need if I'm to fit my house into it.

31. Slowing the Juggernaut: A Servant Approach to Social Change

Many people give checks to save the children, but meanwhile they're giving their lives to the system that is killing the children. And that's crazy. But I suppose it's more convenient than becoming a suffering servant.

But how can servant living change the system? How can it challenge the juggernaut? Personal repentance does not automatically change the system. Institutions have a life of their own; so institutional change is a two-step process. First, people must change, and then those changed people must go to work to change the institutions. If good people do nothing, evil institutions will remain intact.

Recognizing this, the standard approach is to organize good people to lobby for good causes and vote for good candidates. Meanwhile since oppressed people are oppressed because they aren't as well organized as their oppressors, good people must also register the oppressed, get them out to the polls, train them how to work for their rights. All of this is right.

Up to a point.

As I said, institutional change is a two-step process, and this takes care of the second step—getting good people organized. But let's not forget the first step—getting bad people to change, or (as Jesus put it) to repent. Voter education in the ghettoes is essential, but why does no one ever talk of voter repentance in the suburbs? What we need most is more good people so we have someone to organize.

It is a monument to our spiritual poverty that even Christian political activists reduce social change to a technical problem of organizing when what is needed is fundamental spiritual change. Whatever happened to talk of good and evil, costly discipleship, spirituality, repentance, turning our backs on self-interest in order to serve those whom the wicked are oppressing? Surely that is our political agenda, and organizing is secondary—especially since we don't seem to have grasped the spiritual nature of the agenda we should be organizing around.

The heart of the matter is turning our backs on self-interest and calling others to do the same. To become servants. So standard self-interest politics just won't do for Christians; to organize primarily around self-interest is heathen. Yet we go around urging people to oppose the bomb on the grounds that it is not in their self-interest: Even if the United States "won" a nuclear war we would all die in the ensuing nuclear winter, we say.

Do you mean to tell me that nuking everyone in the Soviet Union would be okay providing we survived ourselves? No, so we need to move toward a model of suffering servanthood where we would refuse to nuke our enemy even if it meant our country would be seized. Of course, we should point out the likely outcome of any nuclear war but more as an example of evil's ultimate insanity and insatiable love of death than as a pragmatic calculation against the bomb.

Somehow we've got to move from self-interest to servanthood. Otherwise we won't put out any of the fires of evil; we'll only displace them or force them underground.

Or consider discrimination against black Americans. If the easing of discrimination is not accompanied by an altered moral consciousness, if discrimination is eased only because of pressure blacks applied themselves, then we better watch out. The full force of discrimination will return as soon as blacks let down their guard, and in the meantime the displaced prejudice will pop out against Hispanics, women, or homosexuals. And blacks who make it in the system will join the oppressor class.

If you remember the Vietnam era, most of the protesters

were young men of draftable age (and their girl friends); so the protest was in their own self-interest. I do not object to the selfishness of the protesters, but I do object to the selfishness of those too old to be drafted and therefore too old to protest.

Why is it that our sense of justice is so much more acute when we stand to lose personally? I was rather late opposing the Vietnam war; don't you suppose that that had something to do with my protracted educational deferment? And my kids don't have an especially intense commitment to justice, but if one of them gets less ice cream than the other, they'll take on Goliath hand to hand.

So selfishness is deep. We can't deal with it overnight; in fact the mere idea of dealing with it is ludicrously utopian. Yet that is what Jesus requires of us. And it must be the heart of our personal and political agenda. We must have the spiritual depth and patience to work at it in our own lives and politics, and to call others to that same liberation.

Witness for Peace is a prototype of that sort of Christian political action. It has long-term volunteers in Nicaragua who document the murder, rape, and kidnapping by United States-funded terrorism (the news media certainly do not document it). It calls Americans to repentance.

What is more, the volunteers are in principle prepared to put their bodies between the terrorists and their victims (not exactly in their own self-interest, you must admit). Why don't thousands of us (who have no selfish stake in who wins in Nicaragua) go stand on its borders blocking the terrorists with our bodies? Why don't we infiltrate Afghanistan and block the Soviets the same way?

So the first ingredient of a servant approach to changing the system is to focus on the spiritual roots of injustice. Injustice is not a technical problem but one that grows out of our evil selfishness. And the solution is not so much political organizing as it is evangelism.

"Repent, for the kingdom of heaven is at hand" (Matt. 4:17).

I am fully aware that in places the tone of this book is offensive. Talk of the system and the juggernaut is not likely to win friends. Yet I have chosen to use such language. I have chosen to use it because I believe that most of us need to be jarred out of our easy acceptance of the vile social order that surrounds us. Most of us believe that the political and economic system we are used to is reasonably good and fair; oh, it's not perfect, nothing will be till Christ returns, but all that's needed is a few adjustments, a little tinkering.

My own view is that our system is a juggernaut. It crushes forty thousand kids a day, grows fat selling cigarettes and bombs, installs mind-numbing programs on television, and encourages a climate that destroys marriages. Inevitably, the lifeblood of this system, those who keep it going, are good, decent people—only they block out reality.

Of course, many parts of the system are fine. Some of the services for the handicapped, for example, are marvelous, and certain aspects of education are excellent. And our freedom is unparalleled. Even the system itself is vastly preferable to anarchy or to warring city-states or technologically impoverished tribes.

Yet at the heart of it all is the spirit of the age: Behemoth—terribly corrupt and adding poison to almost everything. Take sex, for example. Sex is one of God's most wonderful gifts, yet the system turns it into the Miss America pageant, sex shops, soap ads, *Playboy*, Harlequin novels, abortion clinics, and divorce. Behemoth runs sexually rampant through fashion, down the beach, on television, and in the macho psyche.

It is this whole spirit of the age that we must challenge. We must name it something shocking like Behemoth or the juggernaut. Otherwise, it will lull us into complacency and blindness. It is important to demonstrate against the bomb and blast the Miss America pageant, but we must be fully aware that they are only symptoms. The disease is the spirit of the age—Behemoth.

And this disease is within ourselves as well as in the system.

So the second element of a servant approach to social change is a deep sense of the vileness of the world's political and economic systems. They are all terribly fallen. Failure to see that is often one of the key weaknesses of the liberal, reformist approach (not to mention, of the conservative approach). But that also raises a key weakness of the countercultural approach: its optimism. The counterculture hasn't quite grasped that the fall is not just something that affects us because of fallen social structures; it is deep within ourselves. So if we do build new structures, they too will be terribly fallen.

I love the idea of someday having a war and no one coming. Or of Exxon being unable to find anyone willing to be its president. But I'm afraid these are dreams.

People won't drop out to that extent till Jesus comes. There will always be plenty of people ready to say yes to the system, plenty of sinners fool enough to go to war. As an approach to institutional change, nonparticipation is inadequate. Confrontation is also needed.

It is important to notice the amount of defiant confrontation in Jesus' approach. That is a third element of a servant approach to social change. In some cases, those who drop out are content to do their own thing and do not bother to confront evil the way Jesus did. Jesus was always into it with the Pharisees. And later the apostles did not need to check out the hotel accommodations in the cities they visited; they stayed in the jails. Whether they set out to do so or not, they constantly made trouble. Behemoth noticed them and didn't like what he saw.

It should be that way with us, too. I don't know whether we should court confrontation, but if we don't find it, it should find us. Christians who haven't spent the night in jail are not in the tradition of Jesus and his disciples.

Our lives should be so different that we find ourselves in conflict with the system and its laws all the time. Behemoth is so vile that we should naturally be telling him no with regularity. If the texture of our lives is one big yes to God, it will be one big no to Behemoth. The time must come when we say with E. E. Cummings, "there is some s. I will not eat"[1] [sic].

Saying no may take the form of being arrested for protesting the bomb or for obstructing United States policy in Nicaragua. It may mean being unwilling to pay war taxes or being unable to vote because all the candidates look like Goliath. It may mean trashing a sex shop or a "Christian" bookstore, breaking windows at the Crystal Cathedral or failing to stand for the national anthem. But for serious Christians it will mean something.

I myself suspect that the most substantial no is the no to money and success. (And, of course, it's really a yes to life.) It challenges Behemoth in institutions, and it challenges Behemoth in ourselves. If we are unimpressed by money, if we are not attracted by status, if power has no hold on us, then the system has lost—at least with us. And the result will be fury.

I have often wondered why living on a little is so divisive. I'm sure it's partly because those who have mastered the technique make others feel inadequate (and that's no virtue). I'm sure it's also partly because those who live on a little have a terrible tendency toward Pharisaism. But I think (or hope, anyway), that it's also partly because living on little strikes at the heart of the system.

Money is what makes the world, or rather the cage, go 'round and those who are immune to it are free to do as they please. And that infuriates those caught in the cage. They want everyone to run as insanely as they do; that way they can believe that the cage is a necessary part of reality rather than something of their own choosing. ("Nothing else is *practical*.") So those who say no are treated as nasty, troublemaking hypocrites.

They are treated as sacreligious. Which makes sense if money is your God. When idolatry is challenged, the idolators become vicious. And that is true whether they worship money, the flag, the political process, or military might.

During one presidential election, I couldn't decide which candidate to vote against; so I reluctantly didn't vote. The outrage that this action produced in many has left me wondering ever since whether I had unintentionally kicked over an idol and should keep doing it.

But does that kind of defiant dropping out change the system? Young Americans fleeing to Canada to escape the draft had a limited effect. They weren't defiant enough. But if enough had stayed home and still said no, the jails might have gotten full enough that the system would notice. Or if opposition to the bomb were intense enough now, keeping it might be too much trouble. Scrapping the bomb might be cheaper than building more jails.

Maybe the reason that individual change hasn't brought much institutional change is that individuals haven't changed much. We haven't changed enough to say no to the institutions. We have not become defiant dissenters like Jesus.

But Christians can't help but say no to idolatry. And when we do, the juggernaut has to slow at least long enough to spit on us. Or to squash us.

But beware. We mustn't take the system too seriously. That is the fourth element of a servant approach. Behemoth likes to think of himself as an octopus with the globe wrapped in his tentacles. But finally he's a pathetic little creep. God laughs at him. And so should we.

If we take the system too seriously, even by fighting too intensely, it will subtly take over our lives. And we'll find ourselves working to lower the price of cocaine so the poor will have equal access. Soon we'll be working for a woman godfather in the Mafia. (Would she be called a godmother?) Or we'll want to integrate houses of prostitution. Or we'll try to divide the pie more fairly with minorities, forgetting that it's arsenic pie. And how about a chairwoman for the Joint Chiefs of Staff?

Sometimes the thing to do is to ignore the system. Not ignore it the way the nightly news ignores the forty thousand children, but ignore it the way Jesus ignored Herod (and sometimes Pilate and the Sanhedrin). Jesus wouldn't acknowledge their sovereignty—for God is sovereign. All the others could do was kill him.

In C. S. Lewis' space trilogy there are creatures called "eldils."[2] They are a sort of angel. When human beings meet them, their idea of the perpendicular changes. What before seemed tilted, now seems straight-up-and-down. In their presence, rooms seem to tilt. They are so powerful that they overwhelm our sense of gravity, our spatial orientation.

The system does that to our values, unless we orient ourselves by Jesus.

We must choose. Will we take the system seriously? Or Jesus?

The system did not set Jesus' values. He owed it no allegiance. It had no power over him. He didn't react to it. He didn't even give Herod the courtesy of being rude. He simply couldn't bring himself to take it seriously.

Someone has said that the greatest threat to any system is children and fools who don't take it seriously. That may be an overstatement, but there's something to it.

If a lame, black woman were asked to be president of Exxon, I don't know what she should do. But I wish she'd laugh (like God)—or not get around to answering.

Many of the values and institutions of our society are so bizzare that clowning seems the only response.

Or silence. Or a fit of giggles.

We should at least try it.

That would be beating Goliath with a yo-yo.

7. BUT HOW?

32. I Never Wanted to Be a Servant

A couple years ago, I spent a month in Asia, mostly with people who had servants. And I didn't like what I saw. It gave me a sense of what servant living would be like.

I don't want to be a servant.

Servants are people who drive you to restaurants and sit in the car while you eat.

Servants are people who run in from the next room to get the salt for you because it's a foot out of your reach. They wash your dirty underwear by hand. Sometimes they sleep in a closet or on the floor in the hall.

And they always carry the luggage, which was a problem when I was there because I travel with a backpack—a heavy one—and the servants never knew how to carry it. So they bruised their shins, and somewhere in Asia there's probably a servant who has a hernia from trying to lug my mysterious backpack. It would have been easier, especially on my self-respect, to carry it myself—but they wouldn't hear of that.

Jesus talked a lot about being a servant, but it's not a job I'd ever want.

The essence of being a servant is not existing. If you're a servant, you do all sorts of jobs without anyone ever noticing that you exist.

Whenever I visited a new house during my trip to Asia, I was introduced around (I existed). But a few people were left out. Eventually I realized that they were the servants. They do not exist.

During the whole month I was introduced to servants by name in only one home.

I was told about a discussion on evangelism in a wealthy church. One woman said she knew so few people who weren't Christian that she didn't see how she could evangelize, and the other people agreed. Finally an outsider asked if most of their servants were Christians. After a silence, the answer came: "I never thought of them." Servants don't exist.

Servants are people who . . . no, servants aren't people. They don't eat—at least not with you. They don't sleep—at least you don't need to provide them with a bed. They're nameless—at least you don't have to introduce them. They don't even have souls—at least you don't think about their spiritual state.

As C. S. Lewis wrote of the Victorian era (in one of the worst sentences ever penned), "Everyone had lots of servants in those days."[1] Think about that. The literal implications of the sentence are that even servants had lots of servants (which is nearly self-contradictory). But what Lewis means is that everyone who was *anyone* had lots of servants. And servants weren't anyone; they didn't even exist.

Remember Huck Finn's line when asked if anyone was hurt in an explosion? "No'm. Killed a nigger." Which is about what a servant is.

Servants, like blacks, don't exist. Or at least, they aren't supposed to.

In our day, "everyone" has servants too, of course. The servants are women. (How else would this manuscript get typed?) Men know that women exist, but we don't see them when they're serving us. Bosses seem to need people who become invisible.

But I don't want to be like them—I don't want to be a servant. I don't mind stuffing envelopes or even cleaning the toilet (though if I did it all the time I'd doubtless change my mind).

But I *do* want to exist. When I've stuffed four thousand envelopes, I want someone to say "Thank you." I want someone to acknowledge my existence.

But Jesus knows about being a servant. Once he asked if a master "thanks a servant who does what is commanded?" (Luke 17:9). Jesus realized that not thanking servants is par for the course. You don't have to thank a person who doesn't exist. That means Jesus not only told us to be servants; he also knew what he was asking.

I never wanted to be a servant. It's not my idea of self-fulfillment.

It's not that I need important jobs, at least that's not the heart of my objection to being a servant. And I don't think I'd mind obscurity all that much. Visibility has its rewards, but they are counteracted by the pressures of responsibility and criticism. (Who wants to tell colleagues that their work is unsatisfactory, and who wants piles of negative letters to the editor?)

What is more, not having to be a big wheel is a relief. It is exhausting to strive for approval, to long for the limelight, to criticize others for your own advantage. Emily Dickinson had a better vision:

> I'm nobody! Who are you?
> Are you nobody too?
> Then there's a pair of us.
> Don't tell—they'd banish us, you know.
>
> How dreary to be somebody!
> How public like a frog
> To tell your name the livelong day
> To an admiring bog![2]

So not being (or rather, not needing to be) a big wheel is a relief. It frees you to be human. You can concentrate on what counts: on human relationships, your family, on oppressed people. You needn't bother to croak your name to an admiring bog.

I'd like being that kind of servant. You're not a big wheel (thank goodness), but you do exist. I wish that's what Jesus meant by being a servant.

But Jesus had other ideas.

Not only did he assume masters don't thank their servants. He also said servants who have been out plowing all day shouldn't expect to sit down and eat when they're done. Rather they have to serve dinner to their masters, who may not even have been working. Not till their masters are through will they be allowed to eat (Luke 17:7–8).

So when you're tired and burned out from working for others, being a servant means serving one more time. It means serving someone who may be a creep.

Or try this for size. The disciples were arguing over who was the greatest, and Jesus told them that the great are the ones who serve (not the ones who want recognition). And as if that's not bad enough, he added that he came to give his life as a ransom for many (Matt. 20:20–28; Luke 22:24–27). He clearly meant that we are to give our lives, too.

The Bible often connects servanthood with the crucifixion. Paul writes about Jesus taking the form of a servant and then proceeds to say that he was obedient to death, even death on a cross (Phil. 2:7–8). And Paul tells us that we're to have the same mind (Phil. 2:5).

Not very fulfilling.

So I don't want to be a servant, and I don't much care if Jesus, Paul, John, Isaiah, and everyone else tell me I should. I'd hate it if my job was not to exist. And I'm in no hurry to get crucified.

I'd rather find a balance—a balance between servanthood and self-fulfillment.

Too bad Jesus never did.

33. By Grace

We live in the belly of the beast.

He feeds us on power, money, and self-fulfillment. So it's hardly surprising that we're not enthusiastic about being servants. I'd rather be anchorman on network news, or win a Nobel prize. Success is what I'm enthusiastic about. I may be relatively immune to money and power, but I'd sure like to be a well-known Christian writer.

We're in the belly of the beast.

How do we change all that? How do we get as enthusiastic about serving as we are about being comfortable or important?

Not by feeling guilty, but by drinking from the spring of living water.

Some people will probably read this book as a list of things they must do. They'll see it as setting goals they must strive and struggle to achieve. But striving to lift yourself by your bootstraps is not the spirit in which this book is written. It is not intended to be a bunch of prohibitions. Rather, it's intended to be a declaration of independence. If it's a list, it's a list of freedoms. We don't have to be slaves in the belly of the beast.

We are free. Free to serve God and others.

That is a promise.

I am not talking about our earning our way to heaven by selling our possessions. I am not talking about justifying ourselves before God. I am talking about God freeing us from the slavery of power, money, and self-fulfillment.

If we admit that we are doing awful things with our lives and if we decide to follow Jesus, then God forgives us. God forgives us through the death of Jesus: by grace. The forgive-ness is free. (At least it is for us; it wasn't for Jesus.) Forgive-ness does not depend on our striving and struggling.

Of course we do strive and struggle, but not for salvation. That's already taken care of. By grace. And we don't need to strive and struggle for God's approval. That we already have. By grace.

In the Garden of Eden we rebelled against God. We chose to leave the path of life and enter the belly of the beast. Hence the horrors—the forty thousand children, the bomb, the sexual distortions, the arrogance, all that.

You couldn't blame God if God chose to abandon us. We have had plenty of chances. After, say, the time of Solomon, it would have been reasonable to leave us to kill each other off. I think that's what I'd have done. The roads are just too deep with corpses—the corpses of every sane and beautiful thing.

I wouldn't have sent my son. Not to become a corpse. (If I'd sent him, it would have been with a sword, as a conquering king. Not to join the corpses.) Do you have any idea what it would mean for your son to become a corpse . . . along with all the others?

But God is different. In gracious love, God sent the son. As a servant. To become a corpse.

Now that's grace.

So I don't need to earn my way to heaven. I can't, given the horrors I've committed. But the very idea is silly anyway. God has already made the way free through that corpse.

I don't need to earn God's approval. I can't anyway, given my quiet support for Behemoth. But the very thought of earn-ing God's approval is disgusting when you remember that we already have it. And at such a cost. By grace, we are freed.

Working for someone's approval is slavery. It is demeaning, debilitating, and self-defeating. Teachers who need their stu-dents' approval aren't likely to get it. But those who have ap-proval within themselves are free to do their work well.

It's as with children. Children have to have their parents'

approval if they are to grow and mature; they have to feel it deep in their bones. Children who don't have it will always be struggling, fighting, and testing. Those who have it are free to obey and grow.

So we are free. By grace. And oddly enough what we're free to do is . . . to strive and struggle. We're free to become servants.

It's not that being a servant is on our list of duties. It's that we're overwhelmed by what God did. The mess was so awful that God sent the only son as a servant. Overwhelmed, we want to be servants, too. We want to follow our master.

We're drawn toward the goal. We struggle and strive to get there. Not with the frenetic, ill-natured struggling of someone driven by a taskmaster. Not with the arrogant self-complacency of someone doing good. But with the enthusiasm of someone headed home at last.

And guilt?

Guilt has its place. But it's not a very big place; so I'm worried when people tell me that I make them feel guilty.

But let's be clear: sometimes we should feel guilty. We should feel guilty about the meaningless, evil, and bent things we do with our lives. If we don't, something is wrong with us; our consciences are seared. I can imagine few things worse than not feeling bad about harm we've caused.

So feeling guilty can be a good thing. And I do tell people that unsuspected normal aspects of life are bent and evil. Most people don't think of themselves as having agreed to serve in the belly of the beast. And when they first hear it, if it doesn't make them angry, it probably makes them feel guilty.

It should. If the shoe fits, wear it. If the way we live adds to the oppression of the poor and we're not doing anything about it, why shouldn't we feel guilty?

Guilty is one of God's good gifts. Its purpose is to bring us to the place that we feel that we're sinners. We need to know that in our bones. Without that knowledge we can hardly repent or ask God's forgiveness. We won't see any need to accept God's grace.

And that's the whole point: accepting God's grace. Guilt is not an end in itself or something we should linger in for long. Its purpose is to drive us into the arms of God.

The solution to feeling guilty isn't telling guilty people that they're okay. It's telling them they can be forgiven by Christ's ultimate act of serving.

Then they'll get on with their work. By grace.

We have to come to the end of ourselves. The self-satisfied are not humble enough to throw themselves on the mercy of God. We have to be broken, which may sound like doom—especially in our day, when we are so intent on self-fulfillment and ego-building. We tell ourselves how great we are; we hide our sins and failings even from ourselves. Denying our problems is one of the central problems of our day. It means we can't confront them and deal with them. We can't accept forgiveness. Part of the good news requires a firm grasp of our wretchedness. By itself that's bad news, but combined with God's gracious invitation it's good news. We must have both: harsh denunciation and a declaration of God's grace.

Law and grace go together. Either one by itself is empty and dangerous. Law without a declaration of grace is not gospel; we realize that. Perhaps we are less aware that grace without law is not gospel either.

Revelation 3 combines the two themes perfectly:

You say I am rich, I have prospered, and I need nothing, not knowing that you are wretched, pitiable, poor, blind, and naked. [How's that for harsh?] Therefore I counsel you to buy from me gold refined by fire that you may be rich, and white garments to clothe you and to keep the shame of your nakedness from being seen, and salve to anoint your eyes that you may see. Behold, I stand at the door and knock; those who hear my voice and open the door, I will come into them and eat with them, and they with me. (Rev. 3:17–18, 20)

Thunder and promise are both there. Otherwise it wouldn't be gospel.

Promise. The message of the New Testament is not that we must sell our possessions and become servants. It's that we can. By God's grace we have that power.

Jesus promised.

We're free to serve.

34. And Sometimes I Wonder about Thee

But why do so few people see things that way? Why do so few people understand the freedom in servanthood? Maybe I'm nuts. Maybe I've been sidetracked and can't tell what matters anymore. Maybe money and power *are* what matter. It's hard to believe that everyone is crazy but me.

I'm not being dramatic. I have that conversation with myself once a week. When I was a kid, my dad used to tell about a Quaker woman who said to her husband, "Everyone in the world is strange except me and thee, and sometimes I wonder about thee." The irony of the story impressed me, and even given my arrogance, I'm still rarely able to persuade myself that I know better than *everyone* else.

So it's only a couple days a week that I manage to believe what I'm saying in this book.

The problem is simple. I live in the belly of the beast. Almost everything around me clashes fundamentally with Jesus. My friends, TV, my education, the books I read, newspapers, ads, my peers—they seldom take Jesus seriously.

I'd like to think that I got my values from studying the Bible, by thinking things through and feeling how others feel, by opening myself to the wind of the Spirit. But that's not how people get their values as a rule.

We get them from other people, by osmosis.

TV, books, and lectures have a limited effect. The values we take on are the values of those around us. First, we absorb the values of our parents. Then the values of those we consider peers. Even teachers don't have much effect. It's colleagues and friends that count. We catch their values unconsciously, like we catch their colds. We don't have to follow a thought process. Rather we catch the spirit.

The only question is, what spirit?

The radical Christian solution is simple: form a church community; make your own culture to counteract the effect of living in the belly of the beast; find a bunch of people who are seeking the mind of Christ so you can support and encourage each other.

There's a lot to that. In fact, I think it's essentially right.

The trouble is, it hasn't usually worked in practice. People in church communities struggle all right, but usually they aren't struggling to find the mind of Christ. Usually they're struggling to cope with somebody's obnoxious personality—quite possibly their own. Or perhaps they're splitting ideological hairs, or fighting over whether to take on yet another project. So on average people who join a community get about as much support as though they'd joined a cat fight.

The fact is that community is at least as much a drain as it is a source of support. And it's not that I've had an unusually bad experience of community. My experience has probably been better than average.

I don't know of any communities that don't have a legacy of damaged personal relations. Even when things are going well, routine maintenance of community is a major chore. Communities are like marriages. They can be wonderful, but even at the best of times they're a lot of work. And often they crumble, with tremendous human damage. It's hard enough to maintain a marriage between two people; you can imagine the problems among twenty or a hundred and twenty people. We human beings are hard to live with.

We are especially hard to live with if we're the sort of people who are so disenchanted with society that we try to retreat by joining a community. The fact is, such people are often professional misfits. Soon they're disenchanted with the others in the community. It's like someone marrying for the third time. It might work, but don't hold your breath.

"Everyone but me and thee, and sometimes I wonder about thee."

So do we give up on community and acquire our values by osmosis from our fellow workers at Exxon?

I think not. Church, after all, is taken seriously in the New Testament. And we *do* need some sort of support group to encourage us in our values.

At one time my wife and I lived in a prosperous suburban community. By making a conscientious effort, we lived on less than our neighbors. But it was hard. Then we moved to a seminary where no one had money, and we soon saw that previously we'd had far more than we needed. At the seminary, people weren't expected to have a different suit for every day of the week, and they didn't go out for pizza every other night. The pressure was off. Almost at once we began living on much less. And it was easy, it was spontaneous—like catching a cold.

When that happens, you don't ask if you're crazy. You just see that you can believe Jesus after all. I've had it happen again and again, when I've had a support group.

But that support group doesn't have to look like a traditional commune, or like the church in Jerusalem at the beginning of Acts.

We don't have to move into a big old house with another family and two singles. We don't have to have a common purse. We don't have to tell people everything they do that annoys us or that we think is wrong.

What we need is support, especially in the areas that we find difficult. And that requires space. We have to leave space for ourselves and others. People have to have room to disagree. They have to feel genuinely free to be and do as they see fit, or they won't be able to give genuine support.

I don't know all that that means, but I think that part of

what it means is that communities shouldn't be quite so intense, quite so inflexible. We need more communities but less demanding ones. (Many of them within standard churches perhaps.) By less demanding, I don't mean as undemanding as standard churches. The most that they demand is that you come once a week to listen to a sermon and look at the back of other members' heads. And not commit adultery (though sometimes they can even accommodate themselves to that). But that isn't being the body of Christ. Church is not meant to be a spectator sport.

Church community must be a place where people are deeply involved, where they know each other enough to give support—and to make some demands. Church community must be a place where Jesus is taken seriously. But then we have to leave some room for people to understand Jesus in their own terms. It should be a place where people can feel supported if they sell their home—or buy a home.

It's a balance that's hard to find, that we all have to find ourselves. And probably never quite will.

Our basic support needs to come from our church communities. But since these are never perfect, we'll need to find some of our support elsewhere.

Take Joe Peterson. Joe Peterson is crazy. He's so crazy that he believes Jesus. He lives in community (the intense kind). They're so poor that they could collect food stamps if they wanted to. They don't seem to worry about tomorrow. (At least, they don't have reasonable plans.) And they're enthusiastic about it.

I don't see Joe very often. (I wouldn't want to; he's too crazy.) But he's an essential source of support for me. I need to see him once in a while to catch his enthusiasm—to have him reinforce kingdom values for me.

We all need a network of support. No church community can provide it all for us.

Your network may include people you see once a month,

when you really talk. Or only once a year when they come see you on vacation. Or it may be conferences you go to from time to time. In one place you may get help with life-style, and in another with worship. In yet another political analysis. (No one has it all together.)

In the Northwest of the United States, they have something called Radical Discipleship Camps. Twice a year people from all over the Northwest get together to discuss kingdom values, or so I thought when I was invited to speak. Halfway through my time, I realized they weren't there to hear me; they were there to play volleyball with each other.

The speakers didn't matter much. All these people were together escaping Exxon. They were holding hands with each other walking out of the belly of the beast.

And that's what we really need to do.

35. Sabbath Rest

Yet I think something is wrong here. My portrayal of serving is too grim, too far from the joys of God's creation. We may not be called to take care of ourselves, but we are called to rest. And resting and serving are closely linked in Scripture.

If we serve all the time and never rest, we are making an understandable mistake. (At least I find it understandable—I make it all the time.) But serving without rest is no more following Jesus than is resting without serving.

The underlying theological principle is Sabbath rest. The biblical mandate for it is overwhelming. It first appears at the end of the creation story: "God blessed the seventh day and hallowed it, because on it God rested from the work of creation" (Gen. 2:3). Sabbath rest is part of the creation order, embedded in the earliest theology of the children of Israel. The Sabbath also appears in the Ten Commandments, another part of Israel's most ancient theology (Exod. 20:8-11). Deuteronomy and Leviticus expand the meaning of Sabbath to the point that faithful observance would mean resting nearly a third of the time: the Sabbath day, the Sabbath year, the year of Jubilee, Passover (eight days), the feast of tabernacles (eight days), a harvest festival (one day), New Years day (one day), the day of atonement (one day), and each new moon (thirteen a year).

Rest and worship were built in to God's creation.

Yet, for many of us, Sabbath is a drab idea at best. And at worst it is another item to add to our list of oughts and no-nos. We think of Sabbath observance not as a means of refreshment but as a way of spoiling our fun. Isn't the idea that you do only those things you can do in your Sunday best? That is, no swimming, lawn mowing, or cycling, though checkers may be okay and Bible trivia certainly is.

But that isn't what Sabbath observance is about. It is about not working all the time. We don't have to be servants twenty-four hours a day, seven days a week; sometimes we're free to rest, to do nothing.

That is what the Bible teaches. I love the verse in Exodus: "On the seventh day you shall rest, that your ox and ass may have rest and the son of your bondmaid, and the alien, may be refreshed" (23:12). At the least this is early legislation on labor rights, not an item on a list of no-nos. And actually that understanding is only a minor part of the meaning. The meaning goes much deeper—this passage is about spiritual refreshment, springs of living water.

Ezekiel makes the same point. After talking about the Sabbath, he refers to God's "ordinances, by whose observance people shall live." And Isaiah says it even better. If you honor the Sabbath,

> Then you shall take delight in the Lord
>   and I will make you ride upon the heights of the earth;
> I will feed you with the heritage of Jacob your father,
>   for the mouth of the Lord has spoken. (Isa. 58:14)

Delighting in the Lord is what the Sabbath is all about.

In Jesus' time legalism was well on its way to killing delight in Sabbath rest. Not taking too many steps was about all that was left. So Jesus fought the Pharisees tooth and nail. He knew what delight in the Lord meant, and he wanted to restore it. He kept tangling with the Jewish leaders over the Sabbath. Finally, he told them, "The Sabbath was made for people, not people for the Sabbath" (Mark 2:27).

In Luke Jesus seems to take the idea of Sabbath rest to a new height. He picks up a theme from Isaiah about the year of Jubilee. It's Jesus' inaugural address kicking off his ministry.[1] It's a declaration of his mission—to bring Sabbath rest to the oppressed and hurting:

The Spirit of the Lord is upon me
and has anointed me to preach good news to the poor.
The Spirit has sent me to proclaim release to the captives
and recovering of sight to the blind,
to set at liberty those who are oppressed,
to proclaim the acceptable year of the Lord. (Luke 4:18–19, quoting
   Isa. 61:1, 2 and 58:6)

So Jesus' mission was to inaugurate perpetual Jubilee—with justice and Sabbath rest for the poor!

The book of Hebrews clearly promises Sabbath rest. In the wilderness the Israelites were offered Sabbath rest, but they didn't believe God could give them Canaan, so that generation never entered God's rest (Heb. 3).

But "we who believe enter that rest" (Heb. 4:3). It does not say that we *can* enter it, or that we *should,* or that we *will* when we die or when Jesus returns. It says simply that we do enter that rest. The verb is not imperative. It is not future. It is not subjunctive. It is present indicative.

The rest that we are promised is the very rest that God took after creation: "So there remains a Sabbath rest for the people of God; for those who enter God's rest also cease from their labors as God did" (Heb. 4:9–10).

It doesn't sound like Christian political activists.

It sounds more like grace.

"Cease from their labors" (Heb. 4:9).

To me that is a staggering thought which shows how much I need it. I don't know how to cease from labor. And I think I'm typical in our culture. Perhaps that's why we find the idea of Sabbath so drab. Wouldn't it be boring not to work? And it doesn't sound very effective either. We don't know how to relax; so we watch television instead. Or go to Disney World. Or drink.

I read recently of a man teaching meditation in a Christian school.[2] The parents objected. Not because it was Eastern or anything, but because the kids weren't *doing anything.*

I suppose meditation didn't seem effective. It is, of course. It's very effective. The teacher could have told the parents how well it works. He could have explained that it lowers blood pressure. (It did mine anyway. It helps my proctitis, too.) It also prevents ulcers. And probably eczema. Those are scientific facts—it's been proven. Your brain waves change when you meditate.[3]

Meditation would probably help social action, too. Soon someone will doubtless write a book entitled *How to Do More Social Action through Meditation*. And it would work.

Meditation also increases the rate at which you learn. There's a book on it.[4] And I don't doubt its accuracy.

But somehow that's not the point.

Some may think that all the books on the good effects of meditation are a sign of spiritual renewal. I think they're a sign of the need for spiritual renewal.

Meditation and the spiritual life are not techniques. At least, they're not meant to be. They are spiritual disciplines that reach down to the roots, where springs of living water well up.

Our culture is practical. People jog, not because they like to, but so they can work better. As a result we think of the spiritual life (if we think of it at all) as a filling station. We go there only to get gas so we can go somewhere else. The filling station is only a means to another end. We'd never stop there unless we wanted to go somewhere else. And if we found a station with cheaper gas, or one with quicker service . . . .

But the spiritual life is the end, not the means. Meditation, worship, and rest are the goal. They aren't a filling station where we have to pause to gain power to get where we're really headed. No, they *are* where we're headed. They are home. The Garden of Eden.

Of course, if we do pause to pray, we will gain power and we will get elsewhere more efficiently. But if that's why we do these things, we'll get nowhere. We'll only drive ourselves further and further from home.

You see, we get confused. I do anyway. I think service and

justice are the important things, and worship and rest are to enable me to serve better. They're means. I rest only enough to be able to go back out and serve. Which is exactly backwards.

Worship and rest are the foundation of service and justice. We serve and we work for justice in order to let others enter into God's rest, into the kingdom. We worship and rest as much as we can, pausing only to clear the way for others to join us. You see, the forty thousand children have little rest. We don't want them only to be able to eat. That's not enough—not nearly enough. We also want them to have the bread of life, to enter God's rest.

For them to cease from their labor.

One vital point is that it is God's rest that we are called to enter—not our own. The focus is not on us; it is on God. We aren't taking care of ourselves; we're worshiping God.

That is a very different focus from that of the standard Christian theologies of self-fulfillment and self-esteem. And it's very different from the standard utilitarian approach of our culture. In this one step, we overcome our culture's narcissism and pragmatism, and we do it without collapsing into asceticism.

On those rare occasions when I worship deeply, something important happens. Though I don't realize it at the time, I forget about myself. My petty concerns (Am I making a fool of myself? Is my hair combed?) disappear. My moral worries (Did I speak too harshly?) are also forgotten. And my anger dissipates. I wonder if that isn't partially what Jesus meant by "Those who lose their lives for my sake will find them" (Luke 17:33).

Forgetting about ourselves in worship makes it possible for us to forget about ourselves in service. Worship and rest are the foundation.

But there is even more to it.

Ceasing from our labor doesn't mean sitting on our duffs all the time. We will still work hard. After all, we're on a war footing. Of course, we'll take at least every seventh day off and for that day not be everyone's servant. But most of the time we'll be out serving. Perhaps my Puritan upbringing is surfacing, but the command to rest on the Sabbath also includes a call to work the other six ("Six days you shall labor" [Exod. 20:9].) There's work to do. The fields are white for the harvest.

Jesus' example carries weight with me. He spent time away from the crowds, alone with his disciples, especially the ones he felt closest to. He went to parties. And he prayed—a lot.[5] He also visited the wilderness and walked in the hills and along the lake (the Sea of Galilee is beautiful). You see, he was teaching about his father, and he kept in touch, so to speak. But that's not all he did. Mostly he worked. He worked himself silly. He taught, he healed, and he confronted the Pharisees.

But even when he worked, he had (I suspect) ceased from his labor. There's a striking phrase in Hebrews. It tells us to "strive to enter the rest" (4:11). A paradox—we are to strive not to labor.

So how do we work yet not labor? I don't know how to explain it, probably because I have so little experience of it, but I think you can work without laboring at it. It happens when you're working freely, because you have springs of living water welling up within. You're not serving out of duty, nor are you angry because you'd rather be doing something else. You're not earning your way to heaven; you're not struggling to accept yourself or trying to gain power. Deep in your bones, you have a sense of God's gracious goodness and your own acceptability. Your effectiveness is not too important to you, so failure is no big deal. You know in more than your head that everything depends on God, and you expect God's intervention.

When you believe these things, you are working freely, without laboring at it. Sabbath rest is yours seven days a week.

In my daily journey, I sometimes find myself worshiping and resting. Sometimes I find myself at the spring of living water. Not often, but sometimes. Then I can work without laboring. I can serve and serve and serve. Then I can paint someone's house without underlying anger that I'm not teaching philosophy.

Mary found the spring of living water. Martha did not—she was too busy serving. Meanwhile Mary was sitting at Jesus' feet, which made Martha angry, of course. Busy servers have a lot of anger, especially if they can't find the spring.

But Jesus told Martha that Mary had chosen the good part, the only part that was needful. And you know what that was, don't you? It was sitting at Jesus' feet.

And I think you will probably find the spring while sitting, especially if you're sitting near Jesus. But I'm not confident how to find the spring, even for myself. Sometimes it seems a long way off. And your route won't be the same as mine.

But when you're there it will be a time of Jubilee. Did you know that the year of Jubilee began on the day of atonement? It was not a "secular" holiday; it was a holy day, a spiritual event. It was a day when sins were forgiven. But it was also a day for politics and economics, for in Israel those things were not separated. Not only were people freed from slavery as the Jubilee began, they were also freed from their sins. Not only were they forgiven their moral debts, they were also forgiven their economic debts. Sin, slavery, debts—spirituality, politics, economics—they are all one at the spring of living water. We are free at last. We can have Sabbath rest the whole year.

But we won't want to come alone. With us, we'll bring the forty thousand children. You see, they have little rest. We don't want them only to have food. That's not enough, not nearly enough. We also want them to come to the spring of living water.

To enter God's rest. That is what we all need.

Appendix
God's Special Concern
for the Poor

Throughout Scripture, you find a special concern for the poor. It varies in its intensity and in whether it includes a special suspicion of the rich and powerful, but that special concern is always there. At times this concern points toward the poor and weak as an ideal, and weakness begins to be portrayed as the force to stop evil. This concern for the poor suggests a class consciousness, and at times it develops into that.

Genesis, which shows as little concern for the poor as any book in the Bible, still shows a concern. It is more impressed with the wealth of Abraham, Isaac, Jacob, and Joseph than it is disturbed by the suffering of the oppressed. But God's statement to Cain could be emblazoned on the flag of all those opposing oppression: "The voice of your brother's blood is crying to me from the ground" (Gen. 4:10). And I love these words after Abraham abandons his young son, Ishmael: "The child lifted up his voice and wept, and God heard the voice of the lad" (21:16, 17). Even the wrathful elevated God of early Israel could hear children cry. God was also sensitive to women, which was not common in that culture: "Jacob loved Rachel more than Leah, and when the Lord saw that Leah was hated, the Lord opened her womb. But Rachel was barren" (29:30, 31).

From Exodus on, concern for the weak and poor is more central. The Exodus story itself is the story of the liberation of oppressed people, and this central event made it natural for

Judaism to be concerned about oppression. The people were often reminded: "You shall not oppress a stranger; you know the heart of a stranger, for you were strangers in the land of Egypt" (Exod. 23:9; see also Deut. 10:19, 16:12, 24:22, Lev. 19:34).

This concern for weak and downtrodden people is expressed concretely in all the legal codes found in the Pentateuch. In the Covenant Code (Exod. 20:22–23:33), nearly a third of the verses protect slaves, the poor, and the defenseless. They aren't all what I would choose. (For example, they limit slavery but don't abolish it, and they view women almost as property, albeit property with rights.)

But at their best they are very fine indeed. They protect strangers, orphans, and widows (Exod. 22:21–24; 23:9). They provide early labor and animal rights legislation by limiting even their workweek to six days (23:12). They prohibit taking interest from the poor or holding their clothes as surety (22:25–27). And every seventh year the Israelites were to free their slaves and leave the land unplanted that the poor and "the wild beasts may eat" (23:11). (But this concern for the poor did not extend to perverting justice for their sake; see 23:3, 6, 8).

The Deuteronomic Code also contains many laws to help the poor and oppressed. Many of them repeat Exodus (Deut. 1:16–17; 5:14; 10:18–19; 16:14, 18–20; 24:17–18; 27:19). Others expand on Exodus: the Israelites not only weren't to charge interest, they were also to be generous (15:7–11). And the law about the seventh year is extended: on it all debts were to be forgiven (15:1–3).

New laws are also added. When harvesting, the Israelites were to leave some of the crops for the poor to pick up (24:19–22). A tithe was to be given the Levites and the poor (14:28–29; 26:12–15). Laborers were to be paid promptly (24:14–15). Weights and measures were to be honest (25:13–16), and stones marking property lines were not to be moved (19:14).

It goes on and on. Some of the laws are lovely: escaped slaves were not to be returned (23:15–16, which is a lot better than the Dred Scott decision of the United States Supreme Court); criminals were not to be degraded by being given more than forty stripes (25:3); the blind were not to be misled (27:18); and, attending to even the smallest detail, oxen were not to be muzzled while treading out grain (25:4).

The Holiness Code goes further. Leviticus 25 legislates economic revolution by requiring land to be returned to its original owners every fifty years. In an agricultural society this amounts to a periodic redistribution of wealth, and not surprisingly, it was probably never practiced. But it shows a depth of concern for the poor, a bias against amassing wealth, and a tendency toward social leveling.

The Law, the fundamental book of Judaism, was passionately concerned about the defenseless. No such concern was expressed for the comfortable and wealthy.

The Prophets carry on the tradition. Their concern for the poor is even more passionate than the Law's. Of course, justice is a moral and spiritual matter, not some kind of secular politics in a separate compartment. Judah and Israel have turned their backs on God, and the chief signs of their spiritual failure are idolatry and oppression of the weak.

I could not possibly catalog all that the Prophets say about the poor and oppressed, but I will detail the class consciousness which begins to emerge in some of the Prophets (reaching full bloom in Luke and James). These Prophets are concerned about oppression, and quite naturally the poor and the weak are not in a position to oppress; it is the strong who oppress. While their message is addressed to all the Israelites, the focus is on the princes, priests, elders, rulers, judges, kings, and rich people. The poor are never singled out for harsh words, though sometimes common people are mentioned as being as bad as their rulers.

Amos is an example. He was a Judean prophesying to Israel at a time of prosperity and security, but he prophesied the destruction of the prosperous. He had harsh words in a pleasant time. Those prosperous enough to have a "summer house" and a "winter house," those who live in "great houses" and "houses of ivory," are the objects of his wrath (3:15). He makes no exceptions; all those in great houses are promised destruction with no hint that those who got their houses "fairly" will be let off. All rich people are tarred with the same brush.

Prosperous women get called "cows of Bashan" (14:1-3); their servants and poor neighbors do not. Amaziah, the chief priest, is told that his wife will become a harlot (7:17). Denunciation is focused on those who build houses of hewn stone (5:11), on merchants who sell to the poor (8:4-6), on those at ease (6:1) on beds of ivory (6:4) anointing themselves with fine oil (6:6). Then in one brief line Amos extends his criticism to ordinary people (probably not poor people): "The great houses shall be smitten into fragments, and the little houses into bits" (6:11). Clearly the brunt of Amos's attack is on those with great houses.

Micah took much the same stance. His message is directed to all the people, but when he gets specific he attacks "you heads of Jacob and rulers of the house of Israel" (3:1, 9) "who eat the flesh of my people and flay their skin from off them and chop them up like meat in a kettle" (3:3). (The people are not the sinners but the sinned against.) Micah's diatribe continues against prophets and priests (3:5, 11). Then he says, "Your rich men are full of violence" (and now an attack on ordinary people) and "your inhabitants speak lies" (6:12). Princes, judges, and great men—"the best of them is like a brier" (7:3-4). And everyone else is equally violent (7:2) and unreliable (7:5-6).

Nor will God use Israel's might to solve their problems. In fact, God is going to destroy their horses, their chariots, and their strongholds (5:10-11) which are put in the same category as sorcery and idols (5:12-14). The solution will come rather from God who will raise up a messiah from little, insignificant Bethlehem. God will save a remnant, and it won't be a collection of rulers and the great; it will be the lame and the rejected

(4:6–7). God has a special concern for the little people. And a special suspicion of the strong and the rich.

Ezekiel's message is also addressed to the whole house of Israel but focused on the elders (8:1; 14:1; 20:1) and the princes (7:27; 11:1; 12:10–13; 17:1–21; 19:1–14; 21:11–12, 25–27; 22:6, 23–31; 45:8–9; 46:18). He makes devastating attacks on the important people: "Each of the princes of Israel uses his power to shed blood" (22:6). But that does not mean common people are let off. In Chapter 22, Ezekiel flays the princes, the priests, the prophets; then he says, "Her princes are like wolves tearing the prey, shedding blood, destroying lives to get dishonest gain. The people of the land [apparently not the poor] have practiced extortion and committed robbery; they have oppressed the poor and needy and have extorted from the sojourner without redress" (22:27, 29).

A class consciousness is beginning to emerge.

Later Ezekiel compares Israel to sheep, where some drink clear water and eat good grass but foul it for others: "Is it not enough for you to feed on the good pasture that you must tread down with your feet the rest of your pasture? Must my sheep eat what you have trodden?" (34:18, 19). "I will seek the lost, and I will bring back the strayed, and I will bind up the crippled, and I will strengthen the weak, and the fat and the strong I will destroy" (34:16; the text of the last word is in dispute). "I myself will judge between the fat sheep and the lean sheep. Because you push with your side and shoulder and thrust at the weak with your horns, I will save my flock and judge between sheep and sheep" (34:20, 21, 22).

For Ezekiel, being fat is proof all by itself of guilt.

This class consciousness is not nearly as clear in the other Prophets. No sign of it can be found in Jeremiah. He is egalitarian: Great and small are equally wicked (Jer. 5:4–5; 6:13; 16:6; 31:34; and maybe 9:23).

But the general tenor of most of the Prophets is rejection of the mighty and support for the weak.

In two of the Prophets, this budding class consciousness develops in a natural yet surprising way. Just as the rich are suspected of wickedness, the poor are presumed to be righteous and pious. Part of the reason is that might is linked with arrogance and therefore with not trusting the Lord, while poverty is linked with humility and relying on God. The Lord's people are the poor and the weak, the meek and the blind.

Zephaniah's quarrel is with "the officials and king's sons and all who array themselves in foreign attire" (1:8). He attacks wealthy "traders" (1:11) and the "mighty" (1:14), and he predicts doom for "the fortified cities" and "lofty battlements" (1:16). Jerusalem's officials "are roaring lions; her judges are evening wolves that leave nothing till morning. Her prophets are wanton," and "her priests profane what is sacred" (3:3, 4).

That is how Zephaniah talks to the powerful. But his tone changes when he addresses the little people: "Seek the Lord, all you humble of the land; seek righteousness, seek humility; perhaps you may be hidden" (2:3). And in the end Israel will be restored:

> I will remove from your midst
>   your proudly exultant ones,
> and you shall no longer be haughty
>   in my holy mountain.
> For I will leave in the midst of you
>   a people humble and lowly.
> And I will save the lame
>   and gather the outcasts. (3:11, 12, 19)

Micah says much the same thing: the inhabitants of the new Jerusalem will be the lame and the rejected (4:6–7). This special place for the lame is all the more striking because Leviticus prohibits lame priests from making offerings; those with defects were not acceptable (Lev. 21:16–24). But in Zephaniah and Micah, those with defects are the ones God accepts.

In the Psalms the story is much the same. Many Psalms (the laments) call God to free the afflicted from their oppressors. In them the children of Israel, the poor, and the righteous are ranged against wicked and arrogant oppressors. The oppressors imagine that God pays no attention, but the weak and the righteous throw themselves trustingly on God who has promised to hear their cry. Other Psalms praise God for having already delivered the oppressed and do so in much the same terms.

Naturally the words for the poor, the righteous, the afflicted, and those who trust God tend to merge; the terms become nearly interchangeable. The poor *are* the righteous; the afflicted *are* the ones who trust God. You're reading a Psalm that seems to be about the righteous, and suddenly it's talking about the poor without signaling a new topic. Then it turns to the children of Israel, then to those who trust God, then to the afflicted—all without seeming to change the subject.

Psalm 14 is a good example. It starts with the fool saying in his heart that God will not see what he's doing. But:

Have they no knowledge, all the evildoers
   who eat up my people as they eat bread,
   and do not call upon the Lord?

There they will be in great terror,
   for God is with the righteous.
You would confound the plans of the poor,
   but the Lord is their refuge.

O that deliverance for Israel would come out of Zion! (14:5–6, 7)

On one side are evildoers who do not trust God and don't think they'll be called to account. On the other are my people being eaten like bread: the righteous, the poor, and Israel. And the poor as a class are said to take refuge in the Lord.

Psalm 22 is much the same. It starts by the Psalmist asking where God is: "My God, my God, why have you forsaken me?" (v. 1). The Psalmist is in trouble (vv. 12–18) but will soon praise the Lord:

You who fear the Lord, praise God!
All you children of Jacob, glorify God!
For God has not despised or abhorred
the affliction of the afflicted;
and God has not hid from them
but has heard when they cried.

My vows I will pay before those who fear God.
The afflicted shall eat and be satisfied;
those who seek the Lord shall praise forever. (vv. 23, 24, 25, 26)

Once again the Psalm intertwines the righteous and the afflicted. The sequence is those who fear the Lord, the Israelites, the afflicted, those who fear the Lord, the afflicted, and finally those who seek the Lord. The mixture is amazing.

The merging of the poor and the pious also happens in Psalms 69, 86, 94, and 140 and to a lesser extent in 10, 74, and 123. In fact, all the laments take on a deepened meaning if you read them realizing that those who first used them identified the oppressed with the righteous. (See also Ps. 72:2 and 107:35–43.)

In Psalms 146 and 147 something comparable happens. These hymns of praise stress complete trust in God. They contain these verses:

The Lord sets the prisoners free,
the Lord opens the eyes of the blind.
The Lord lifts up the bowed down;
the Lord loves the righteous. (146:7, 8)

Prisoners, the blind, the bowed down, and the righteous are all in the same category.

The Lord watches over the sojourners,
the Lord upholds the widow and the fatherless;
but the way of the wicked the Lord brings to ruin. (146:9)

The Lord lifts up the downtrodden,
the Lord casts down the wicked. (147:6)

The wicked are contrasted with sojourners, widows, the fatherless, and the downtrodden, and that clearly implies that the unfortunate are not wicked.

This is a reversal of the standard Old Testament view that the righteous are wealthy, and it is a reversal which leads to a new kind of piety. What matters is not wealth, prosperity, and power, but humility, meekness, and a drastic dependence on God. Wealth and power tend to be contrary to such virtues, and so poverty and weakness are the ideal.

God's ideal.

Notes

CHAPTER 1: I DON'T UNDERSTAND

1. James P. Grant, *The State of the World's Children: 1981–82* (New York: UNI-CEF, 1981), p. 1.
2. Kenneth Patchen, "Have You Killed Your Man for Today?" and "Eve of St. Agony or The Middleclass Was Sitting on Its Fat," *Selected Poems* (New York: New Directions, 1957), pp. 53, 56.
3. Anthony Trollope, *Barchester Towers* and *The Warden* (New York: Modern Library, 1950), p. 170.
4. William Neil, *The Difficult Sayings of Jesus* (Grand Rapids, Mi.: William B. Eerdmans Publishing Co., 1975), pp. 4–5.

CHAPTER 2: INSANITY

1. Grant, *The World's Children: 1981–82*, p. 1.
2. Samuel Clemens, *The Adventures of Huckleberry Finn* (New York: Grosset and Dunlap Publishers, 1948), p. 281.
3. U. S. Bureau of the Census, *Statistical Abstract of the United States, 1985* [Washington, D.C., 1984], p. 446.

CHAPTER 4: THE DOORWAY TO LIFE

1. Malvina Reynolds, "The Magic Penny," (New York: Northern Music Co., 1958).

CHAPTER 9: OBSCENITY

1. See also Ps. 123:4; Zech. 1:15; but contrast Isa. 32:18 and 33:20. Luke 12:19 is another interesting verse to compare.

CHAPTER 10: ON NOT WASTING YOUR LIFE

1. Of the 558 verses in Luke where Jesus is teaching, at least 108 of them (19 percent) are about possessions, and another 20 may be. Of the total 1147 verses in Luke, at least 126 of them (11 percent) are on possessions.

2. We spent $6.6 billion on candy in 1984 (U.S. Bureau of the Census, *Current Industrial Report on Confectionary, 1984* [Washington, D.C., 1985], p. 2), and $864 million worth of chewing gum was sold wholesale in 1983 (U.S. Bureau of the Census, *1983 Annual Survey of Manufacturers* [Washington, D.C., 1984], p. 2/5). In 1983 Americans claimed $31 billion in tax deductions for giving to religion (U. S. Bureau of the Census, *Statistical Abstract of the United States, 1985* [Washington, D.C., 1984], p. 385), and only 5 percent of that went overseas (David B. Barrett, "Silver and Gold Have I None: Church of the Poor or Church of the Rich?" *International Bulletin of Missionary Research* 34 [October 1983]: p. 149).

3. In 1983 Americans spent $28.3 billion on tobacco and $51.4 billion on alcohol (U. S. Bureau of the Census, *Statistical Abstract of the United States, 1985* [Washington, D.C., 1984], p. 435). That year U.S. foreign economic aid was $8.7 billion, one third of which was loaned and not given (ibid., p. 796).

4. George Thomas Kwian, ed., *Encyclopedia of the Third World*, vol. 3 (New York: Facts on File, 1983), p. 2028.

CHAPTER 11: THE DANGER OF POSSESSIONS

1. Luke 5:29–35; 7:36–39; 11:37–41; 13:1–24; 15:1–32; 19:1–10.

2. See also Exod. 23:23–33; Lev. 26:1–45; Num. 14:6–9; Deut. 27; Josh. 7:1–26; 24:19–20; Judges 2:1–5, 11–23; 3:7–30; 4:1–23, passim; 2 Sam. 21:1–6; 2 Kings 17:5–20; 21:1–16; 2 Chron. 36:11–21; Ezra 9:10–15; Neh. 13:15–18; Isa. 1; Jer. 2; Ezek. 5, 34; Hos. 4; Joel 2, Amos 2, Obad., Jonah, and almost all the rest of the chapters in the Prophets—with the possible exception of Daniel.

CHAPTER 12: SELL YOUR POSSESSIONS

1. In Mark the strand is there, but it is minor. Mark has the story of the rich young ruler (10: 17–31) and of the poor widow (12:41–44), but since Mark is an action book, it doesn't have extended teaching like the Sermon on the Plain or the reply to the man concerned about his inheritance. If we had only Mark, conscientious Christians would be wondering about possessions, but the tendency to ignore this strand would be less surprising.

The strand is in Matthew much more clearly than in Mark, though not as clearly as in Luke. Matthew has the cluster of sayings that would lead to not having possessions if followed (5:40, 42), the better part of a chapter warning against possessions (6:19–33), the saying that Jesus has nowhere to lay his head (8:19–20), the parable or the sower in which "the delight in riches choke[s] the word" (13:3–23), and the story of the rich young ruler (19:16–31). Besides, Matthew adds the two parables about the treasure buried in a field and the pearl of great price (13:34–35).

Matthew also has the calls to the disciples (4:18–22; 9:9–13) but omits that they left everything, and his version of Jesus' warning to seek the kingdom and not be anxious about food and clothes does not culminate in "sell your possessions" (6:25–33). He does not have the story of the poor widow giving all; his Beatitudes have less reference to possessions (5:3–11); and he doesn't have the saying about renouncing possessions or the long teaching in reply to the man concerned about his inheritance.

CHAPTER 14: SHARING

1. For other Old Testament passages, see, for example, Ruth 2:1–23; Neh. 8:10–12; Est. 9:22; Job 22:7–9; 31:16–20, 31–32; Ps. 112:5, 9; Prov. 11:24–25; 19:17; 31:20; Ezek. 16:49.
2. For other passages in the Gospels on sharing, see Matt. 6:2; Mark 9:40; Luke 3:10–11; 10:29–37; 14:12–14; 16:19–31.
3. See Ronald J. Sider, *Rich Christians in an Age of Hunger* (Downers Grove, Ill.: InterVarsity Press, 1977), pp. 98–103.
4. A whole series of other passages in the Gospels focus on renunciation without mentioning the poor. See, for example, Luke 14:27, 33; John 12:24–25; Matt. 16:24–26; Mark 8:34–37; Luke 9:23–25; Matt. 10:37–39; Luke 17:33.

CHAPTER 15: MONEY IS NOT ENOUGH

1. See also Exod. 23:6; Deut. 10:18; 23:16; 24:14–15, 17–18; 27:19; Lev. 19:13; 25:14, 17.
2. See also Job 22:8–9; 24:2–4; 29:12; 34:28.
3. See, for example, Ps. 9:9, 12; 14:4, 6; 22:24; 25:16; 44:24; 55:2, 11; 69:32; 73:6, 8; 76:9; 79:11; 82:3–4; 94:6, 20; 102:20; 103:6; 109:16; 119:107, 122, 134; 140:12; 146:7; 147:6.
4. See also Prov. 1:10–19; 6:16–17; 11:16; 14:31; 15:25; 21:13; 22:16; 23:10–11; 28:3, 5; 29:14; 31:4–5, 8–9.
5. See also Amos 2:6–8; 5:10–12, 15, 25
6. See also Isa. 1:23; 5:7–10, 23; 10:1–4; 14:4; 30:12; 32:7; 33:15; Mic. 2:8–9; 3:1–3, 9–12; 6:6–8, 10–12; 7:2–4; Hos. 4:2; 5:10; 6:9; 12:6–8; Jer. 2:34; 5:26–28; 7:5–7; 9:6; 17:11; 20:13; 21:12; 22:13–17; Ezek. 13:19; 18:7–8; 22:6–12, 25–29; 34:15–24; 45:8–9; 46:18; Zeph. 1:9; 3:1–3; Zech. 7:10; 8:16; 11:4–7; Mal. 3:5.

CHAPTER 16: PROPHETIC EVANGELISM

1. Thomas Middleton, "Light Reflections: How the Other Half Talks," *Saturday Review* 6 (Jan. 20, 1979): p. 16.

CHAPTER 17: STRUCTURAL CHANGE OR CULTURAL REVOLUTION?

1. Paul is not popular with many radicals, and I understand why, but I suspect his writing is the source of much radical thought—even thought that attacks him.
2. C. S. Lewis, *The Silver Chair* (Harmondsworth, Middlesex: Penguin Books, 1965), p. 200.
3. A standard objection is that you can't expect the world to live by the ethics of the kingdom, and so it doesn't make sense to try to pass laws to make non-Christians act like Christians. I, however, am inclined to draw the opposite conclusion: since non-Christians don't naturally follow kingdom ethics, we need laws that will encourage them to do so in hopes of making true life more possible. Our primary task, of course, has to be inviting people to join the kingdom (evangelism) so that they will live kingdom ethics spontaneously, but I see no reason not to also try to pass good laws.
4. Will D. Campbell and James Y. Holloway, *Up to Our Steeples in Politics* (New York: Paulist Press, 1970).

CHAPTER 18: A QUESTION OF CLASS

1. See, for example, Matt. 4:23–25; 5:1; 8:1, 18; 9:8, 33, 36; 11:7; 12:23, 46; 13:2, 34, 36; 14:13–21, 35; 15:10, 30–39; 17:14; 19; 20:29; 21:8–11, 14–15; 23:1.
2. See Matt. 3:7; 5:20; 9:3–7, 10–13, 34; 12:1–8, 9–15, 22–32, 38–42; 15:1–20; 16:1–4, 5–12; 19:3–9; 21:14–16, 23–46; 22:1–14, 15–22, 23–33, 34–40, 41–46; 23:1–39; 26:3–5, 14–16, 47–68; 27:1–2, 3–10, 12, 20, 41, 62–66; 28:11–15.
3. Lev. 12:6–8.

CHAPTER 21: GOD

1. The various codes of the law make the same point. See Exod. 20:2; 23:27; Deut. passim but especially 7:7–8; 9:6–7; and all of chapter 28; Lev. 21:22–26; 26:8, 36.
2. See also 2 Kings 19:17–19; 1 Chron. 5:20; 11:14; 14:15; 17:7–8; 18:6; 2 Chron. 6:24; 13:15–18; 14:11; 16:7–9; 18:31; 20:12–15; 24:24; 25:8; 26:14–16; 32:7–8; Ezra 8:22; Neh. 4:4, 9, 14; and all of Esther.
   The poetic books are equally repetitive about God's strength being what matters. (See Job 12:7–25; 40:10–14; Prov. 15:25; 21:31.) The Psalms focus on our human dependence on God's strength: the hymns in the Psalter extol God's greatness till people seem small (see Ps. 8, for example); the songs of trust express Israel's trust in God rather than themselves (Ps. 62); the sacred histories tell how God delivered Israel despite their weakness and sin (Ps. 78); the laments tell of terrible troubles and ask for God's help because people certainly can't help themselves (Ps. 3); the songs of thanksgiving thank God for deliverance (Ps. 30); the wisdom Psalms teach that God is the only important thing (Ps. 1). This deliverance and help is not something

vague or metaphysical: every fourth Psalm has military imagery calling God something like a shield, a stronghold, or a fortress (see Ps. 3, 7, 9, 18, 27, 28, etc.). We tend to see deliverance as something metaphorical that God does for our souls, but Israel saw it as military salvation from the likes of Egypt and Assyria.
3. See also Isa. 2:12–22; 10:13–16; 20:1–6; 22:8–11; 30:15–16; Jer. 1:4–8, 18–19; 5:17; 9:23–24; 17:5–8; 48:7; 50:33–38; 51:10, 20–23; Hos. 1:7; 7:11; 8:14; 10:13–14; 13:4–6; 14:1–3.

CHAPTER 22: THE CROSS OR THE SLINGSHOT?

1. See Acts 5:1–11; Rom. 13:4; Rev. 19:14–21.

CHAPTER 27: JOBS AND KINGDOM WORK

1. C. S. Lewis, *Voyage of the Dawn Treader* (Harmondsworth, Middlesex: Penguin Books, 1965), p. 177.

CHAPTER 28: MODEL ONE: WILL THE REAL ALLIGATOR PLEASE STAND UP?

1. John Keats, "Ode on a Grecian Urn," *The Complete Poetry and Selected Prose of Keats*, Harold E. Biggs, ed. (New York: The Modern Library, 1951), p. 295.

CHAPTER 31: SLOWING THE JUGGERNAUT: A SERVANT APPROACH TO SOCIAL CHANGE

1. E. E. Cummings, "i sing of Olaf glad and big," *Complete Poems: 1913–1962* (New York: Harcourt Brace Jovanovich, Inc., 1972), p. 339.
2. C. S. Lewis, *Out of the Silent Planet* (London: Pan Books, 1952); C. S. Lewis, *Voyage to Venice, or Perelandra* (London: Pan Books, 1953); C. S. Lewis, *That Hideous Strength* (London: Pan Books, 1955).

CHAPTER 32: I NEVER WANTED TO BE A SERVANT

1. C. S. Lewis, *The Magician's Nephew* (New York: Collier Books, 1970), p. 76.
2. This is the version I memorized in high school: Emily Dickinson, "I'm Nobody! Who Are You?" *Adventures in American Literature*, fourth edition, Rewey Belle Inglis, Mary Rives Bowman, John Gehlmann, Wilbur Schramm,

eds. (New York: Harcourt, Brace and Company, 1951), p. 734. Apparently it is not quite the original: for that see Thomas H. Johnson, ed., *The Complete Poems of Emily Dickinson* (Boston: Little Brown and Company, n. d.), p. 133.

CHAPTER 35: SABBATH REST

1. Scholars are not completely unanimous, but something close to a consensus is emerging that Jesus is here proclaiming a year of Jubilee. After all, "proclaim release to the captives" is similar to "proclaim liberty throughout the land," which is the language used in Leviticus 25:10 to introduce the Jubilee year. Besides, the year of Jubilee is a reasonable candidate for being "the year of the Lord." Finally, in Jesus' time the Essenes thought that Isaiah was refering to the year of Jubilee (See Robert Sloan, Jr., *The Favorable Year of the Lord* (Austin, TX.: Schola Press, 1975).
2. Tilden Edwards, *Spiritual Friend* (New York: Paulist Press, 1980), p. 69.
3. Herbert Benson with Miriam Z. Klipper, *The Relaxation Response* (New York: Avon, 1976).
4. Sheila Ostrander, Lynn Schroeder, Nancy Ostrander, *Superlearning* (London: Souvenir Books, 1979).
5. See Mark 1:35; 3:7, 13; 4:35–38; 6:31–34, 45–47; 9:2–8, 30–31; 10:10; 14:17–42.

Index of Bible Verses